Where Eagles Fly!

"But those who wait on the Lord shall renew their strength; They shall mount up with wings like eagles…" (Isaiah 40:31)

by

Dr. James Lee

As the Lord goes with you wherever you go,
His divine presence and glory will overshadow you
and protect you all the days of your life!

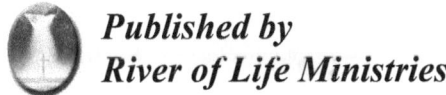

Published by
River of Life Ministries

Copyright © 2025 by Dr. James Lee

Where Eagles Fly!

Be strong and of good courage; for the Lord your God is with you wherever you go.

by Dr. James Lee

Printed in the United States of America

ISBN 978-1-7342549-7-6

All rights reserved solely by the author. The author guarantees all contents are original and do not infringe upon the legal rights of any other person or work. No part of this book may be reproduced in any form without the permission of the author.

Unless otherwise indicated, Bible quotations are taken from New King James Version of the Bible. Copyright © 1982 by Thomas Nelson Inc. The Scriptures of the Bible are the main references of this book.

www.rlmva.org

ACKNOWLEDGEMENTS

I would like to acknowledge my Lord and Savior, Jesus Christ and to give all the glory to Him who inspired me to write this book so that many lost, suffering, and struggling souls can be encouraged by the grace and love of God.

"Bless the Lord, O my soul, and all that is within me, bless His holy name!" (Psalm 103:1)

I would also like to acknowledge our friend and Messianic Jewish sister, Laura Kotrosa who spent many hours to edit this book and one of my disciples, Elizabeth Rooney who formatted and created the covers for the book.

Lastly but not least, I would like to acknowledge my dear wife, Margarita for encouraging me to keep on writing this book when I was struggling to move forward with receiving God's inspiration for the next chapter.

Finally, I give all the praise to the Holy Spirit who endorses and inspires me to write this book for God's glory.

CONTENTS

Acknowledgements..v

Introduction...vii

Chapter 1
One Life to Live...11

Chapter 2
Live an Expectation Free Lifestyle................................37

Chapter 3
Shake off the Viper...60

Chapter 4
Arise and Shine; for Your Light Has Come...................83

Chapter 5
Be a Miracle Maker in Christ.......................................103

Chapter 6
Be More Than a Conqueror...125

Chapter 7
Be a Victorious Follower of Christ...............................138

Chapter 8
Mount Up with Wings Like Eagles...............................153

INTRODUCTION

We are truly living in the Last Hour of the Last Days according to Matthew 24:6-7, *"And you will hear of wars and rumors of wars. See that you are not troubled; for all these things must come to pass, but the end is not yet. For nation will rise against nation, and kingdom against kingdom. And there will be famines, pestilences, and earth-quakes in various places."* As we watch the current news, we witness the signs of the end times unfolding right in front of our very eyes. One of the signs that Jesus Christ prophesied was pestilences.

For example, from January 2020 to May 2023, we had gone through one of the deadliest pestilences called—the COVID-19 a pandemic which had been brought to over 180 nations. Tragically, more than one million people in America died from the infection of Coronavirus. It brought great fear into people's hearts and released anxiety about an uncertain future. It caused multitudes of businesses to collapse each day, resulting in unexpected economic downfall in the U. S. and the world. A person focused only on all the negative effects that the COVID-19 pandemic had brought to the world, would be filled with worries, fear, doubt, depression, oppression, and hopelessness generated by the power of darkness.

Now is God's *Karios* (the Greek word meaning God's right, critical, and opportune moment) time that we need to seek Him and begin His new life by repenting of our sinful lifestyle and turning away from our wicked ways (any ways that are not ordained by the Lord and the word of God). We need to pray that His mercy and grace will deliver us from the fear and power of darkness according to His promises in Psalm 91. We need to truly surrender our lives to the Lord Jesus Christ and be guided by the Holy Spirit each day so that we can enjoy victorious and abundant life according to His promises in John 10:10b. If we are truly born-again in Christ, then we need to accept the truth that all our sins have been washed by the blood of the Lamb. We also need to be baptized in the Holy Spirit and His power (Acts 1:8), so that we can be strong and very courageous in Him no matter what we may face in life. We must know how to be like King Hezekiah who encouraged his military captains before the massive invading armies of the kings of Assyria in 2 Chronicles 32:7-8:

> ***Be strong and courageous**; do not be afraid nor dismayed before the king of Assyria, nor before all the multitude that is with him; for there are more with us than with him. With him is an arm of flesh; but **with us is the Lord our God, to help us and to fight our battles**. And the people were strengthened by the words of Hezekiah king of Judah.*

For such a time as this, what the lost, hurting, suffering, and fearful people of the world, as well as the children of God, need to hear is the encouraging words of God penetrating into their hearts to eliminate every fearful voice from the power of darkness. Therefore, we must not focus on the negative, doubtful, and fearful reality of the present dangers like Hezekiah's leaders did, but we must be very strong and courageous in the Lord and allow the presence and power of God to encourage us to move forward into His divine victory as eagle Christians. When Joshua was charged by the Lord to take the Israelites into the Promised Land after the death of Moses, He spoke to him in Joshua 1:9, "***Be strong and of good***

courage; do not be afraid, nor be dismayed, for the Lord your God is with you wherever you go." If the Lord will be with you wherever you go, then you can truly wait on the Lord to renew your strength so that you will mount up with wings like eagles to accomplish His will in your life. As the Spirit of the Lord guides me to write this book, it will identify how some of the heroes of the Bible and in Christ handled their own challenges, despairs, fear, dangers, and defeat by focusing completely on the Lord and His mighty power in all circumstances. It will encourage you to put your absolute trust in the Lord no matter what circumstances may dictate your heart to fear.

Joshua lived in the Old Testament era with the mighty Holy Spirit resting upon him. However, the Lord commanded him to be strong and of good courage because He would be with Joshua wherever he went. With God's presence going with Joshua, he was able to lead the Israelites to conquer the Promised Land for His glory. Since we live in the New Testament era where Jesus Christ and the Holy Spirit reside inside of all born-again believers, we can be assured that the Lord is with us wherever we go.

Therefore, we can also be strong and very courageous to possess our Promised Land for His glory. Furthermore, we need to learn how to encourage ourselves in the Lord just like King David did in 1 Samuel 30:6, "*Now David was greatly distressed; for the people spoke of stoning him, because the soul of all the people was grieved, every man for his sons and for his daughters. But **David strengthened (encouraged) himself in the Lord** his God.*"

As you read this book, you will be encouraged in the Lord knowing that He is always with you and the power of the Holy Spirit will cause you to be strong and very courageous to face any circumstances in life for His glory. You are never alone in this life. The Lord will fight every battle for you as you put your total faith and trust in Him and not on the negative reports of the power of darkness that release fear into your heart. Therefore, we need to wait patiently on the Lord and allow Him to release His promises in Psalm 23:6 to be activated in your life—"*Surely goodness and mercy shall follow me all the days of my life; and I will dwell in the house of the Lord forever."*

Then, the Lord will equip you to be His eagle Christian to accomplish His mission and creation mandate on earth all the days of your life. Eagle Christians will fly over every storm, danger, attack of darkness, sickness, and destruction with the power, grace, mercy, and unconditional love of the Lord all the days of their lives. Eagle Christians are tenacious, courageous, bold, determined, and focused to fulfill God's divine missions in their lives.

Eagles do not fly with other birds but only with other eagles with same mind, spirit, vision, purpose, and destination. They will never quit, give up, or surrender their God ordained Creation Mandates to any distractions, obstacles, hindrances, traps, and snares of the devil along the journey of their lives in Christ. In this book, you will discover how you can apply these principles in each chapter into your lives. So, you can be God's anointed eagle Christian to soar up high into your divine destiny accompanied by other eagle Christians along the journey of conquering your Promised Land for His glory.

Chapter 1

ONE LIFE TO LIVE

We only have one life to live, so we must do everything we can to make it count for the glory of God and to enjoy each moment as His gift for us. What we face in life each day occurs only once and it will never be repeated again exactly the same way it happened, even though you may be confined in the same place with the same people day in and day out. Thus, the Psalmist wrote in Psalm 118:24, *"This is the day the Lord has made; we will rejoice and be glad in it."* God creates each day for us to enter in and we must choose to rejoice and be glad in it no matter what circumstances we may encounter. We have the power to make the day very joyful, filled with life, and blessings or a miserable, defeated, fearful, and tormented one according to how we choose it to be.

We must choose to live each day as though it is our last day on the earth. If you truly know that tomorrow will be your last day, then you will prepare to face your final day as best as you can at least the day before, because the sun will rise the next morning for the last time. If you have not forgiven someone in your heart, perhaps, you will try your very best to get right with that person before the last sunset of your life. If you have not told your loved ones how much you truly love them, then you should call all of your loved ones to let them know your sincere love for them. If you have a final wish to share with your family members, you should carefully and prayerfully decide what to disclose in your final will to them in writing. You may want to repent of all your sins before God and truly accept Him as your Lord and Savior so that you will have eternal life with Him in heaven. You should do everything in your power to have peace with God, others, and yourself before the final hour. You may want to enjoy your favorite meals for the last time on the earth. You may want to see the sun rise and set for the last time...etc. Because the word of God in Hebrews 9:27 states very clearly, *"And **as it is appointed for men to die once**, but after this the judgment."* The Old Testament Scripture in Ecclesiastes 3:17 confirms the notion of the judgment, *"God will bring into judgment both the righteous and the wicked, for there will be a time for every activity, **a time to judge every deed**."* (NIV)

Therefore, God challenges us to choose life in Deuteronomy 30:19, *"I call heaven and earth as witnesses today against you, that **I have set before you life and death, blessing and cursing; therefore, choose life** that both you and your descendants may live."* Whatever the enemy of God, Satan, releases to human beings will always bring destruction and death according to John 10:10, *"The **thief does not come except to steal, and to kill, and to destroy**. I (Jesus Christ) have come that **they may have life, and that they may have it more abundantly**."* If we follow the ways of the devil (symbolically written as the thief), we are allowing death and destruction into our lives; however, if we choose life in Jesus Christ, we will find divine heavenly life and life more abundantly while we are living on the earth.

Ultimately, God provides the best option for every human being to enjoy the one life that we have, but each of us must choose how to live each day for His glory to receive His abundant life. When God created Adam and Eve, He created them according to His image and likeness to enjoy eternal life and to exercise His kingdom power to have dominion over every living thing that moves on the earth (Genesis 1:26, 28). The garden of Eden was an extension of heaven on earth where they were responsible to tend and keep it according to God's perfect will. They were to be fruitful and multiply, fill the earth and subdue it, and have dominion over every living thing as His son and daughter. God's perfect will for Adam and Eve was for them to propagate godly children to fill the whole earth so that His glory, presence, power, blessings, love, joy, peace, and abundant life would manifest through them and their descendants.

Unfortunately, when they listened to the voice of Satan who distorted, lied, and manipulated God's truth and His simple commandment in Genesis 2:17, they lost two blessings of God—1) **eternal life** and 2) **the kingdom authority and power** to have dominion over every living thing on the earth. Consequently, after the fall of man, the descendants of Adam and Eve followed the suggestion of Satan in Genesis 3:4 and chose to be their own gods to decide good and evil for themselves.

Satan became the ruler of this world and the god of this age (John 12:31 and 2 Corinthians 4:4) and every human being began to die on earth and to be cast into the eternal hell fire (Matthew 13:50; Matthew 18:8). The corrupted and sinful blood of the first Adam brought death to all humanity according to Romans 5:12, *"Therefore, just as through **one man sin entered the world**, and death through sin, and **thus death spread to all men**, because all sinned..."*

That means if the corrupted blood (DNA) of the first Adam is flowing through your veins, you will die and will be cast into the eternal hell. Even though one may try to do many good works to acquire the eternal life in heaven, one can never buy one's way to life after death by accumulating self-righteous acts. What is the evidence of the fruit of the sinful DNA of the first Adam? It is described in Galatians 5:19-21, "*Now the works of the flesh are evident, which are: adultery, fornication, unclean-ness, lewdness, idolatry, sorcery, hatred, contentions, jealousies, outbursts of wrath, selfish ambitions, dissensions, heresies, envy, murders, drunkenness, revelries, and the like; of which I tell you beforehand, just as I also told you in time past, that **those who practice such things will not inherit the kingdom of God.**"

You can also identify them in 1 Corinthians 6:9-10, "**Do you not know that the unrighteous will not inherit the kingdom of God?** *Do not be deceived. Neither fornicators, nor idolaters, nor adulterers, nor homosexuals, nor sodomites, nor thieves, nor covetous, nor drunkards, nor revilers, nor extortioners will inherit the kingdom of God.*" Then, what must we do to be saved from the curses of the first Adam's DNA? The answers are in the following Scriptures in the Bible: 1) Leviticus 17:11, "*For the life of the flesh is in the blood, and I have given it to you upon the altar to make atonement for your souls;* **for it is the blood that makes atonement for the soul**." 2) Hebrews 9:22, "*And according to the law almost all things are purified with blood, and* **without shedding of blood there is no remission.**"

According to the above Scriptures, in order for you to be saved, you have to accept the blood sacrifice of the Lamb of God, who died on the cross for your sins, into your heart by asking Him to be your Lord and Savior. You need to accept the fact that Jesus Christ crucified your old man who was under the bondage of the cursed DNA of the first Adam on the cross with Him when you were baptized into His death (Romans 6:3-6). Because your old man is dead in Christ, now you are born-again by inheriting the new DNA of the Last Adam's blood and you will have eternal life in the Kingdom of Heaven and abundant life on the earth.

So, Romans 5:17 assures life through Jesus Christ, *"For if by the one man's offense death reigned through the one, much more those who receive abundance of grace and **of the gift of righteousness will reign in life through the One, Jesus Christ**."* Therefore, God sent the Last Adam—Jesus Christ—to redeem the fallen humanity to have eternal life again by dying on the cross to pay the penalty of sin and death for each descendant of the first Adam. As the Last Adam was resurrected from death, He provided His kingdom authority and power back to every born-again son or daughter to expand the Kingdom of God with signs, wonders, and miracles following to evangelize the unreached peoples, tongues, tribes and nations in the world (Matthew 28:18-20; Acts 1:8; Matthew 10:7-8, 24:14).

Furthermore, God created each person who ever lived on earth to fulfill His creation mandate in one's life as He spoke to Jeremiah in Chapter 1:5, *"**Before I formed you in the womb, I knew you**; before you were born, I sanctified you; I ordained you a prophet to the nations."* God declared to Jeremiah that He knew him before he was formed in his mother's womb. What did God know about Jeremiah before his father and mother had even met each other?

I believe that God knows His perfect creation mandate for each of His created human beings before they were ever formed in the womb. God wrote His creation mandate for mankind in Genesis 1:28, *"Then God blessed them, and God said to them, '**Be fruitful** and **multiply; fill the earth** and **subdue** it; **have dominion** over...every living thing that moves on the earth.'"* There are five things God wanted man to do: 1) Be fruitful; 2) Multiply; 3) Fill; 4) Subdue; 5) Have dominion. These are God's divine purposes for which man was created.[1] God knows His perfect plan for each person to fulfill while living on the earth for His glory. As I traveled to the nations, the happiest, blessed, and most complete people I have met were those who not only knew their Creator, but also were living to fulfill His perfect will in their lives each day. Every person who has ever been born in this world is not created by accident or mistake, regardless of one's circumstances and situations.

However, one may say that he or she was born out of a wedlock or became an orphan in an early age so he or she might feel or was told that he or she was born into this world by accident or mistake. It was, is, and will always be the devil who comes to steal, to kill, and to destroy God's creation mandate in one's life, so one can never know one's true divine purpose and plan without knowing the Creator God. Even many Christians do not know God's divine creation mandate for their lives, and they are constantly wandering in the journey of life to discover their true purpose in Him. Since we all have only one life to live on earth, it is absolutely crucial that we find out what God's perfect creation mandate is for our lives.

DISCOVERING GOD'S CREATION MANDATE

How can we know God's divine creation mandate for our lives so we can be truly fulfilled in living according to His perfect plan and purpose each day? In order to discover God's creation mandate, we must totally surrender our lives, self-wills, desires, and plans to be in line with His perfect will by dying to ourselves. Now, you may think dying to yourself is too difficult for you to do and want to stop reading this book all together. I encourage you to keep reading so that you may truly understand and be set free from many obstacles that you have built around your life that have blocked you from discovering your God ordained creation mandate. Once you know the truth, it is actually very easy to identify your destiny in Christ. If you are in Christ, His divine blessings, life, love, joy, peace, and favor will follow you. God is always victorious, so you will be more than a conqueror in Him. Nothing is too difficult for God. And with His help, you can be victorious too. He can guide you through to victory over any problem, issue, or struggle in your life.[2]

It begins with accepting what Jesus Christ has already done at the cross for us when we give our lives to Him and become a born-again believer. We do not need to work to achieve what Christ has already done for us but to acquire the truth by only believing in faith. If we are in Jesus Christ, the following Scriptures prove that you have already been set free from the bondages of the lies of the devil:

1) **Your old man was crucified with Christ** according to Romans 6:3-6, *"Or do you not know that as many of us as were baptized into Christ Jesus **were baptized into His death**? Therefore, we were buried with Him through baptism into death, that just as Christ was raised from the dead by the glory of the Father, even so **we also should walk in newness of life**. For if we have been united together in the likeness of His death, certainly we also shall be in the likeness of His resurrection, knowing this, that **our old man was crucified with Him**, that the body of sin might be done away with, that we should no longer be slaves of sin."*

The above Scriptures very clearly declare that when we were baptized into Christ Jesus, we were baptized into His death. Because **our old man,** who was under the curses of the first Adam, **has been**

crucified with Christ and is now forever dead so we can be born-again in Him. Thus, we are able to walk in newness of life in the New Adam, the resurrected Lord Jesus Christ, with His divine blessings and life flowing into our lives. We can never crucify our old cursed nature, under the DNA of the first Adam, with our own willpower to set us free. However, religious spirits will torment you by implying that you have not tried enough to crucify your old man on the cross, so you are still suffering under the bondages and curses of the power of darkness.

In reality, we can never deliver ourselves from the curses of the first Adam. If we have the power to free ourselves from the bondages by using our own willpower, then why did the Last Adam come and die on the cross to save us from the curses of the first Adam? God knew that we, the fallen mankind, can never be able to save ourselves from the power of sin, sickness, curse, fear of death, and Satan. So, He sent His own sinless Son to pay the penalty of death on the cross for us. Then, our old man, who committed all kinds of sins, would die with Christ and a new man would be resurrected with Him to live the brand-new life in Him.

Therefore, if we accept the truth in faith that our old man was crucified with Christ when we were baptized in Him, then we can instantly be free from all the curses and DNA of the first Adam. Just like Christians believe in faith that they will go to heaven when their lives are over on the earth because they simply believe the truth of the word of God. So, I pray that you will accept the truth in Romans 6:3-6 and declare that your old man has already been crucified with Christ, so you can be totally free from all the curses of the first Adam. As you claim and accept the truth of what Christ has already done for you, you will be setting yourself free from the works of the law of sin and death once and forever. Now, you are ready to live a new life in Christ.

2) **There is therefore now no condemnation** according to Romans 8:1-2, *"There is therefore now no condemnation to those who are in Christ Jesus, who do not walk according to the flesh, but according to the Spirit.* ***For the law of the Spirit of life in Christ Jesus has made me free from the law of sin and death.****"* If we are in (literally inside of) Christ Jesus, we will have no other choice but to walk according to the Spirit because He always walks in the Spirit. That means, we must believe and accept our position in Christ through faith as the above words of God promise.

It is impossible for us to make ourselves holy by applying our own human willpower to eliminate all our sinful desires like Buddhist people try; or by following the laws in the Bible to be holy like the Pharisees tried; or by separating ourselves from the evil influences of the world like monks and Amish people have done. We can only be truly holy before God by willfully choosing to live inside of Christ every moment of our lives. Jesus Christ is the holy resurrected Son of the living God who allows His sons and daughters to dwell inside of Him so that we can be holy as He is holy. Therefore, Jesus spoke to His disciples in John 14:20-21, *"**At that day** you will know that I am in My Father, and **you in Me, and I in you**. He who has My commandments and keeps them, it is he who loves Me.*

And he who loves Me will be loved by My Father, and I will love him and manifest Myself to him." Jesus Christ states very clearly that from the day of Pentecost (at that day in John 14:20), the unfolding of the New Covenant era, the Holy Spirit came and began to dwell inside of the believers. Therefore, by the indwelling presence of the Holy Spirit, sons and daughters of God will be inside of Christ and He will be in them—this reality initiated the new living temples of God on earth. As we are in Christ as born-again believers, we are able to enjoy His holiness, freedom, power, goodness, faithfulness, love, joy, peace, forgiveness, righteousness, and salvation without any condemnation.

If we are in Christ Jesus, then we can truly enjoy the law of the Spirit of life in Him that will set us free from the law of sin and death (Romans 8:2). Everything that we receive from Christ such as salvation, baptism in the Holy Spirit, deliverance, healing, holiness, righteousness, and peace are His gifts for us, and we can only appropriate them by faith. If you have been working to acquire Christ's life-giving attributes in the past, then you need to renew your mind and receive them by faith.

Then, the rivers of living water will flow out of your heart to discover God's creation mandate for each day to live for His glory. Your one life in Christ can be a gift unto multitudes of others who are dying, suffering, and lost in this world because He will begin to do His work through you as you are in Him. Of course, we must do our part in remaining in Christ no matter what kinds of temptations the devil may send in our path. If we listen to and follow the ways of Satan, then his destructive power of darkness will be activated, and we will fall into his bondages of sin and death. But as quickly as we repent of our sins, quit walking in the devil's wicked ways, and turn back to the ways of Christ by repenting of our sinful lifestyle, He has the power to restore us back to walking in His divine creation mandate to fulfill His will on earth.

3) **You present your bodies a living sacrifice** as Romans 12:1-2 commends, *"I beseech you therefore, brethren, by the mercies of God, that **you present your bodies a living sacrifice, holy, acceptable to God,** which is your reasonable service. And do not be conformed to this world, but **be transformed by the renewing or your mind**, that you may prove what is that good and acceptable and perfect will of God."*

However, in order for us to live each day fulfilling the creation mandate in Christ, we have to present our bodies as a living **sacrifice** (*thusia* in Greek: an act of offering God something precious) unto Him each moment of our lives. Then, the Holy Spirit will have His total freedom to live through us (His earthly temple) and empower us to enjoy His victorious, abundant, and blessed one life to live on the earth.

Once we present our life as a living sacrifice and dwell inside of Christ, then we are truly separating our life unto God's purpose on earth as His holy vessels of honor for His glory. In order to appropriate that, we must not conform to this world and its wicked and evil belief system that is totally contrary to the word of God and His principles for His sons and daughters. We must be God's kingdom citizens on earth obeying His commandments to fulfill His divine plan in our lives for His glory.

Also, we must be transformed by the renewing of our mind by meditating on the word of God and praying in the Spirit each day. Our mind is controlled by our soulish desires that have great tendencies to follow the ways of this world by conforming to secular lifestyles to satisfy our own ways and wills. We would love to choose good and evil for ourselves so that we become gods of our own lives on the earth.

Therefore, we have to renew our own minds to be transformed by the mind of Christ to carry out the will of God on earth as Jesus did before He went to the cross— "*My Father, if it is possible, let this cup pass from Me; yet not as I will, but as You will* (NASB: Matthew 26:39b)." Once we surrender our free will to God's perfect will for our lives, then we will be able to prove what is that good, acceptable, and perfect will of God for our lives.

Then, we will live to fulfill our creation mandate on earth that will release God's glory, love, joy, peace, presence, power, anointing, salvation, blessing, healing, deliverance, and victory to set hurting, dying, lost, and suffering souls free from the power of darkness in the world. Consequently, you will be so fulfilled, happy, completed, and joyful in all you do for His glory with your short life on the earth.

Therefore, we must live to do God's mission in our lives to bring His peace and divine perspective for each circumstance, situation, matter, and person that we encounter every day to fulfill His will and not our will. Then, you will be flying high according to God's perfect will to fulfill His divine creation mandate for your life as a fearless eagle Christian who can do all things through Christ for His glory alone.

LIVE A GOD ORDAINED LIFE (ZOE)

According to the definition in *Vine's Complete Expository Dictionary of Old and New Testament Words*, the Greek word, *zoe* is used in the New Testament as a principle life; life in the absolute sense, life as God has it, that which the Father has in Himself, and which He gave to the Incarnate Son to have in Himself. Living fully for God's glory and fulfilling His will on earth does not mean that you only live a religious, legalistic, and self-induced holy and sacrificial life without having enjoyable and meaningful relationships with your loved ones and other people in your journey of this life.

As I have traveled to over 100 countries to expand the Kingdom of God for the past 37 years, I have unfortunately met many so-called Christian people, who have been bound by religious spirits. These spirits have controlled them with many different legalistic, loveless laws, and traditions that caused them to live a miserable and unfulfilled life without truly enjoying God's divine glory and life for themselves. I also have met multitudes of people living this one life wandering aimlessly without knowing the purpose and plan of the creation mandate of God.

They only live to indulge their insatiable desires of the lust of the flesh, the lust of the eyes, and the pride of life (1 John 2:16). But I also have met numerous fulfilled sons and daughters of God who live according to His perfect will to fulfill their creation mandates in life. **Nevertheless, life can be very unfair and cruel even to God's children after they have surrendered their lives to Him.** We can face all kinds of sufferings, failures, sicknesses, rejections, tribulations, and even the death of loved ones, in this life. When troubles come into our journeys of life, we must not quickly fall apart and begin to question God's love or intention for our life, or even blame Him for not protecting us from the attack of the devil. Instead, we need to be very strong and courageous in God by totally trusting Him in faith no matter what we may go through. We must be assured that He will never leave us nor forsake us. God promised the Israelites (now we are His spiritual Israel—sons and daughters of God) that when they would go through different levels of trials, He promised that He would be with them in Isaiah 43:2:

> *"When you go through deep waters, I will be with you. When you go through rivers of difficulty, you will not drown. When you walk through the fire of oppression, you will not be burned up; the flames will not consume you.* (NLT)"

The same promises of God have been repeated in Romans 8:35, 37-39:

> *"Who shall separate us from the love of Christ?* **Shall tribulation, or distress, or persecution, or famine, or nakedness, or peril, or sword**? *Yet in all these things we are more than conquerors through Him who loved us. For I am persuaded that neither death nor life, nor angels nor principalities nor powers, nor things present nor things to come, nor height nor depth, nor any other created thing, shall be able to separate us from the love of God which is in Christ Jesus our Lord."*

According to the above Scriptures, God is hinting to us that we will go through various trials in life after we become His born-again sons and daughters. As we try our very best to fulfill God's creation mandate in our life, Satan will do everything possible to derail us from obeying God's plan and purpose. Regardless of what various kinds of attacks the enemy launches against us in different forms of trials and tribulations, if our eyes are focused on God, then we can overcome them. Also, God sends the Holy Spirit to help us during our journey of the difficult seasons, to know what to pray for and to know how to pray for it by praying through us (Romans 8:26-27).[3] We need to have absolute faith in Him with a strong and very courageous heart as we go through the valley of the shadow of death.

Then, deep waters, rivers, and fires of oppressions described in Isaiah 43:2 will not harm us because God will go through the tests with us. The Holy Spirit will empower us to be more than conquerors through Christ who loves us. Once we overcome our trials through God's divine grace, then we can boldly declare, *"Who shall separate us from the love of Christ? Shall tribulation, or distress, or persecution, or famine, or nakedness, or peril, or sword?"*

We can do all things through Christ who strengthens us no matter what the devil tries to discourage, derail, depress, or oppress us with his wicked schemes in life as we focus on God's mighty presence, glory, and power to release His life and love to the lost, hurting, dying, and suffering souls in the world. Let me share with you a couple of examples of different lives that I have encountered in the world. They have deeply touched my heart as they have chosen to live God's divine life regardless of all kinds of opposition that they have to face in life. They are true eagle Christians who have learned to fly over every storm which has been sent to their paths by the power of darkness. They are tenacious, uncompromising, never quitting, and determined conquerors in Christ to accomplish what God has established before them to achieve God ordained missions in their lives.

GOD'S REDEMPTION FOR A BROKEN YOUNG COUPLE IN BULGARIA

I met a young devoted Christian leader (I will call him Alex) who was one of the small group leaders of a church in Bulgaria, who was mentoring a young lady (I will call her Tanya) in his group. Tanya was going through the process of divorce. Her husband was a pimp in town who had abused her psychologically and physically according to his wicked and evil desires. However, the leadership of the church forbade Tanya to divorce her husband because they believed God's will for her was to serve her husband no matter what condition she was in. Not only that, they also declared that if Tanya would divorce her husband and marry another man, they would excommunicate her from the church.

Alex counseled Tanya according to the teaching of Christ in Matthew 19:9, if she desired to be freed from her husband due to his ongoing sexual immorality, she would be permitted to divorce him. To make a long story short, Tanya eventually divorced her husband and she fell in love with Alex, the young home group leader. While I was ministering at the church where Tanya was attending, she approached me to ask if it would be all right for her to marry Alex.

I prayed about it and counseled Tanya and Alex to know if their commitment for one another in marriage was truly based on God's grace, love, mercy and forgiveness. They assured me of their true commitment to God and His call upon their lives to fulfill their creation mandates together as husband and wife for His glory. I gave them my permission and prayed for them that God would bless their union with His grace and love.

However, when they announced their intention to get married to the leadership of the church, the Senior Pastor excommunicated both of them out of their church fellowship. Eventually, they got married and they started a new church in another town and became a blessed pastoral team for over 200 young people. When I met them again, they were filled with joy of the Lord and love of Christ for each other as husband and wife and copartners in ministry to deliver many broken young people from the bondages of the devil. They overcame their trials by totally trusting in the Lord that He would walk with them during their tribulations and relied on His grace as they forgave the leadership of the church to rebuild their broken lives.

They were so happy, joyful, blessed, and empowered by fulfilling their creation mandate each day after the marriage. Jesus Christ heals the wounded, hurting, and rejected people and gives them second, third, or even eighth chances to rise up again in order to fulfill their divinely appointed destiny in their lives for His glory. We, born-again believers in Christ, must remember that we all have been saved by the grace of God and also fall short of the glory of God many times during our journey of faith in Christ. Therefore, we must render forgiveness, healing, deliverance, restoration, and the unconditional love of Christ to the fallen, struggling, suffering, and dying humanity by sharing the real Gospel of the Kingdom of God to bring life to them without compromising the truth of the Bible.

In John 10:10, Jesus Christ assures us that He has come so that we may have His divine life [*zoe*: self-existing life of Christ], and we may have it more abundantly. When we surrender our lives to Jesus Christ by accepting Him as our Lord and Savior, He will come into our lives to empower us to have His *zoe* to discover our creation mandate. Then, we can truly enjoy this one life to be filled with His divine love, joy, peace, and purpose to glorify the Father. That's why we are called to share the gospel of Jesus Christ wherever we may go each day so that lost souls can find His life of love, joy, peace, victory, and divine purpose by fulfilling His creation mandate.

A VICTORIOUS LIFE OF A BROKEN COLOMBIAN GIRL

I want to share with you another God-ordained life story. I met an 8-year-old girl, Sherly, at a Christian home for orphans and poor children in Bogota, Colombia in April 1989. I spent a couple of hours getting to know the director and the approximately 24 girls at the home. Before I left the home, Sherly and the other girls came around and prayed for me, my family, and my ministry with very sweet and powerful prayers. When I was about to leave the home, the director asked Sherly to escort me to the main street and help me catch a taxi to go back to Margarita's (my wife's) sister-in-law's home.

She held my hand and walked with me to the main street and helped me to catch a taxi. She told the driver the address where I needed to go, then she waved at me with a big smile and said to me in Spanish, "*Please come back again soon.*" The director of the children's home told me that she was a very good Christian honor student, and a great helper at the home. After that first meeting, Margarita, who is originally from Colombia, and I decided to assist the home financially through our ministry and to help Sherly each month. She had a living mother, brother and sister but she had never met or known her biological father. Her mother decided to keep her sister and

Where Eagles Fly!

brother with her, but put Sherly at the girls' home to take care of her. Over the years, Sherly fell in love with Margarita and I, and she began to call us her mother and father. At one time, we brought Jennifer (our daughter) and Eliezer (our son) to meet Sherly at the home and they also fell in love with her. The director of the home realized that she loved us very much, as though we were her real parents. So, when Sherly turned 14 years old, the director suggested we adopt her so she could have a better life in the United States.

Margarita and I prayed about it and we felt that it was God's will for us to adopt her. We visited Sherly at the home and asked her if she would like to be adopted into our family. She was overjoyed with tears flowing down her face and said that she would love to be adopted into our family as our new daughter. After that, the director of the home arranged for us to meet her biological mother to acquire her approval to allow us to adopt Sherly as soon as all the paperwork was finished in a few months.

She gave us the legal permission and we rejoiced together with the director about our decision to adopt her. We went to the office of the Social Service in Bogota and began to apply for the official adoption papers for Sherly. Within two weeks, to our big surprise, the director of the Social Service in Bogota gave us the approval letter for the adoption. As soon as we came back to Virginia Beach where we lived, we began to apply for the U.S. side of the adoption process for Sherly and it was going very smoothly. But 30 days after Sherly's mother gave us the permission to adopt her, we received a dreadful telephone call from the director of the home in Bogota saying that, according to the Colombian adoption law, the biological mother could change her mind within 30 days and revoke the adoption agreement. Sherly's mother changed her mind and took Sherly with her to the Social Service's office and annulled the adoption process. After that, she took her back to the home and left her there on the 30th day. Sherly, the director, Margarita and I were devastated by the turn of the events. Especially, Sherly was so brokenhearted that she didn't want to talk with anyone for a while at the home. We encouraged her that we would do whatever we could to find a way to adopt her in the future.

But it was not possible before she turned 16, the maximum legal age for a Colombian teenage girl to be adopted into the U. S. We tried to have Sherly visit us as a tourist after she turned 18 years old, but the U.S. Embassy denied her visa application three times. In the meantime, we sent her to a private bilingual school (English and Spanish) for Sherly to learn to speak English. We would take her to vacation places with us in Colombia whenever we visited her during the summertime. During the course of Sherly's difficult journey of life, we encouraged her to trust the Lord and never to blame or forsake Him for what had happened.

We promised her that we would always be her loving parents and never abandon her. We challenged her that though the devil might not want her to have God's divine life, she should furthermore live for God's glory and forgive her birth mother unconditionally. By the grace of God, Sherly never walked away from Him and she drew even closer to Him by going to church to pray at the 6:00 a.m. prayer meetings each morning.

When she turned 18, she told us that we were her only true parents and she wanted to change her last name to have ours. We prayed together and God gave her a new name—Hannah Sherly Lee. We helped her to change her name officially in Colombia and she has been very proud to be called Hannah Lee. We sent her to a school to acquire a special technical certificate and become an endoscopic specialist. She has been working as an assistant to a gastroenterologist doctor in Bogota for many years. In 2017, she contacted us to share her desire to become a fully Registered Nurse, so she applied for the RN program at a very prestigious nursing school in Bogota, and was accepted. We told her that we would do our very best to support her for acquiring a RN degree in the University.

We had been assisting her to finish the school by 2021, but due to the COVID pandemic, her study has been delayed. Finally, she graduated in June 2023. No matter what had happened to Hannah, she never gave up her hope in the Lord or her desire to fulfill His call upon her life. In the spring of 2017, she also told us that she met a wonderful young man, Juan Pablo, who was working at a bank, but he was not a believer in Christ. We told her that it was very important that Juan Pablo be a born-again Christian like her if he seriously desired to become her future husband.

Shortly after the conversation with us, Hannah told Juan Pablo that he should not even think about asking her to go out for a date unless he truly became a true born-again believer in Christ. Otherwise, she would never date him or see him again. So, Juan followed Hannah to her spirit-filled evangelical church whenever she went, including early prayer meetings for two years.

In the meantime, Juan became a sincere born-again Christian. Hannah asked us to come and meet Juan Pablo in September 2018. Margarita and I went to Bogota and met Juan and fell in love with him. We were able to witness that truly God has brought them together for His glory. We gave them our blessing to date and later to become one in marriage in the near future. She also received the approval of the pastor of the church to date Juan. A year later, Hannah and Juan Pablo were married at the church on December 7, 2019.

We were able to take part in her wedding and I had the privilege of praying for them during the service. She was radiant with the joy of the Lord on her face as I walked her down the aisle to release her to Juan Pablo. She would often call to ask us how we were doing during the COVID-19 lockdown season and still to this day she checks up on us often. Hannah is a very strong and courageous young lady who could have been destroyed when she realized that her dream of becoming adopted into our family would not materialize.

However, she forgave her birthmother and decided to live happily and joyfully regardless of her situation. She has chosen to live a God ordained one life on earth for His glory to fulfill her creation mandate with her wonderful husband. Three days before her wedding, she asked me to have a father-daughter date, so I took her to a very nice restaurant for dinner and after that we went to watch a movie.

She was holding my hand as we walked toward the movie theater and she said, "*I love you very much and you are my only father that I have ever known. You have been so good to me, and I will always love you. I would have loved to be adopted to your family, but then I would not have a chance to meet Juan Pablo. God knows the perfect destiny for my life, and I am very happy to fulfill His will for me and Juan together as one.*" I had to use a Spanish translator app in my phone to communicate with her with my broken Spanish and her broken English, but I felt we understood each other fairly well.

Margarita and I thank the Lord for allowing Hannah to be in our lives and we are so proud of her for overcoming all her wounds, rejections, despair, sufferings, and pain to be a very strong and courageous daughter of the King, Jesus Christ. Hannah has joyfully accepted God's creation mandate for her life and His blessings are following her now. Hannah and Juan had their first son, Emanuel, on February 27, 2023. Margarita and I were able to visit them and dedicated Emanuel, our 7th grandson, to the Lord. Hannah is truly an eagle Christian who has been moving by the wind of the Holy Spirit to be a more than conqueror in Christ.

ENJOY GOD ORDAINED ONE LIFE FOR HIS GLORY

I would like to share with you an anonymous note by an *"Old Friend."* The title of a short piece of advice by him was called *"Do not forget to live!"*

"First, I was dying to finish my high school and start college and then I was dying to finish college and start working. Then I was dying to marry and have children. And then I was dying for my children to grow old enough so I could go back to work. But then I was dying to retire. ***And now I am dying…and suddenly realized I forgot to live.*** *Please don't let this happen to you. Appreciate your current situation and enjoy each day. To make money we lose our health, and then to restore our health we lose our money…We live as if we are never going to die, and we die as if we never lived…"*

We must treasure each day as God's gift for us to enjoy our one and only life to glorify Him. It will be a very sad reality if we realize on our death bed that we have forgotten to truly live according to God's creation mandate. As King Solomon wrote in Ecclesiastes 6:1-2, *"There is another serious tragedy I have seen under the sun, and it weighs heavily on humanity. God gives some people great wealth and honor and everything they could ever want, but then he doesn't give them the chance to enjoy these things. They die, and someone else, even a stranger, ends up enjoying their wealth! This is meaningless—a sickening tragedy."* (NLT)

We can work very hard to accumulate wealth during our prime of life in order to live comfortably or even luxuriously after retirement. However, our hard-working accumulated wealth may not necessarily make us enjoy life fully according to our own desires. On the contrary, we can continue to live a miserable and unfulfilled life without experiencing the great joy of discovering our creation mandate.

We can never be satisfied without knowing and fulfilling the purpose and destiny of our life by the Creator God. There is a life of perfect peace, perfect joy, and perfect love that ought to be the aim of every child of God by fulfilling the creation mandate. Such should be the standard for children of God, and they should not rest until they have attained that position. That is God's standard, where He wants all His children to be in Him.[4]

I met a wealthy man one time while I was ministering in a city in Florida who was dying with stage four cancer. He told me that he grew up in a very poor home with four siblings. His parents' situation was so wretched that they were not able to buy him new clothes, so he always got used clothes and shoes from thrift stores. He did not want to live as a poor man like his parents, so he decided to get a college education in mechanical engineering to become a wealthy man.

He also planned to retire at age 65 to buy a very nice summer home in Minnesota and a winter home in Florida to enjoy the latter days of his life without having any concern about financial worries. In order to achieve his goals in life, he worked very hard and sacrificed his whole life for his dream retirement. He only took his family of five (his wife and three children) on vacation every three years just like his parents were able to do for him and his siblings. His whole purpose in life was to be successful and to accumulate wealth so that he can buy retirement homes to enjoy his golden days. Unfortunately, when he turned 61 years old, he was struck with cancer and within a year, it had spread all over his body. Suddenly, he realized that his dream might not be able to be fulfilled, and he became desperate to be healed of cancer so he could live his dream life after the retirement.

When he shared his life story with me, I became very sad in my heart because he had truly forgotten to live just like the man described in Ecclesiastes 6:1-2. He asked me to pray for him to be healed of cancer, but without surrendering his life to the Lord Jesus Christ. I suggested he take his family and grandchildren to a very nice place for two weeks to enjoy some time with them, because he did not have any guarantee of his future. I also asked him to surrender his life to Jesus Christ so he might be healed by His grace. When I told him that, he emphatically stated that he had to be healed first, then he would give his life to Christ.

Once he was healed, then he would retire and build his dream retirement homes for him and his wife so that his children and grandchildren could come and enjoy life with him. Tragically, he passed away shortly after I met him. We must live this one life well for God's glory so that when our time comes, we can say that we finished the race well and the glory of the Kingdom of Heaven is waiting for us. If we are born-again believers in Christ, then we know that He will never leave us nor forsake us. Knowing that reality, we can be strong and very courageous no matter what we may go through in this short life. Therefore, we can encourage ourselves in the Lord as we claim His promises in Romans 8:31, 35, 37 in our lives: "*If God is for us, then who can be against us?...Who shall separate us from the love of Christ? Shall tribulation, or distress, or persecution, or famine, or nakedness, or peril, or sword? Yet in all these things* **we are more than conquerors through Him** *who loved us.*" Once we know that God's love will carry us through all kinds of tribulations in life, then we must live completely for His good pleasure and not for our own, according to Philippians 2:13, "*for it is God who works in you both to will and to do* **for His good pleasure**."

Whatever we do, we need to do it wholeheartedly unto the Lord as we are commanded to do in Colossians 3:23-24, "*And whatever you do, do it heartily, as to the Lord and not to men, knowing that* **from the Lord you will receive the reward of the inheritance**; *for you serve the Lord Christ.*" Let us live this one life well, enjoying every moment by counting it as God's gift. Let us be more than conquerors in Christ over every tribulation that we may face on earth. Then we will become God's eagle Christians to fly wherever He directs us to go to fulfill His creation mandate for His glory.

Eagle Christians must be focused on God ordained destiny for their lives with His divine vision to fly to accomplish His creation mandate, regardless of the obstacles the devil puts before their paths. Eagles are fearless and tenacious when they face the storms coming toward them because their eyes are fixed on the destiny where they are flying to. Likewise, we the eagle Christians must fix our eyes on the Lord Jesus Christ, no matter what kinds of storms we may face during our journey of this one life, and we must only live to fulfill His purpose, plan, and creation mandate for His glory.

Chapter 2

LIVE AN EXPECTATION FREE LIFESTYLE

We have power to make our life filled with joy and blessed by trusting and having absolute faith in the Lord according to His perfect will each day. Or we can allow our life to be depressed, oppressed, miserable, filled with fear, worries, anxieties, doubt, unforgiveness, bitterness, anger, and unbelief because of our lack of faith, trust, reliance, and peace in God's plan and purpose for our life each day.

One of the main reasons why we become so disappointed in life is because of what we expect from our loved ones, friends, coworkers, business partners, or even God has not materialized in the way we desired, or it came very short of our anticipated and expected results. Therefore, Proverbs 13:12 declares, *"Hope deferred makes the heart sick, but when the desire comes, it is a tree of life."* Our hope can be deferred if it is not anchored in the perfect will of God but in our own selfish desires.

The level of disappointment can be measured by the difference between the reality of the outcome and the anticipated or desired degree of our expectations. For instance, you would be very disappointed if what you have been expecting from your loved ones or friends during a time of your great need has been far short of your desired response from them. The level of the gap between your expectation and the reality of the outcome will contribute to the degree of your disappointment. A bigger gap will produce a greater disappointment; a smaller gap will create a lesser disappointment. If you keep your level of expectation from others as closely as you can to the reality of the current situation, outcome, or return from them, then your level of discouragement will be minimized. In other words, if your level of expectation from others becomes as close as possibly to the reality of their status or response, then your disappointment in that matter will be minimized. The hope deferred or unmet expectation will cause your heart to be bitter toward them. Based on your anticipated expectation of their responses can also cause you to be discouraged, frustrated, disappointed, and begin to mistrust them. Your bitterness toward them can also create a judgmental, condemning, and unforgiving heart.

As I traveled to more than 100 countries to minister and counsel numerous people in the past 37 years, I have met so many people disappointed with their husbands, wives, parents, children, siblings, grandchildren, in-laws, friends, co-workers, church members, pastors, leaders, and even God. Their expected outcome from those they trusted has not been sufficiently satisfied according to their hearts' desires. I have witnessed that this has led them to live with sadness, discouragement, unforgiveness, bitterness, anger, condemnation, and judgmental and critical spirits, which open doors to evil spirits to bring curses upon their lives.

There is one word that sums up the effects of a curse: ***frustration***. You reach a certain level of achievement in your life and everything looks set for a bright future. You have all the obvious qualifications—and yet something goes wrong when you are dealing with your trusted people around you! So you start all over again to rebuild new relationships with them, and reach the same level of trust as before, but once again things go wrong. After this happens several times, you realize it is the pattern of your life. Yet you cannot see any obvious reason for it. You might have allowed spiritual curses to be activated in your life by being frustrated over unmet expectations from your loved ones, friends, and even God.[5]

At this point, I would like to make it very clear that what I share in this chapter is totally based on my personal experiences and opinions that have incurred during my upbringing in South Korea, my almost 10 years of serving in the United States Air Force as an officer, and ministering and traveling to more than 100 countries as an evangelist. My main observations and points on this issue are to encourage you to follow the guidance of the word of God and the Holy Spirit, so that you can be free from wrong expectations that can cause you to live a very disappointed, wounded, and hurtful life.

MY OBSERVATION AS A SOUTH KOREAN

I am originally from Seoul, South Korea and immigrated to the U.S. in 1976. I grew up in a home which had been heavily influenced by Confucianism, Buddhism, ancestor worship, superstition, and occultism. My great grandfather was one of the cousins of the last King of the Lee dynasty in Korea, and I was brought up with very strict rules for honoring elders. In those days, generally speaking, children were told to respect and honor parents, grandparents, in-laws, and any other elderly relatives when we would either visit them or they would visit our home.

If I would not get up quickly and greet them properly, I would get into a big trouble for not properly showing them honor. The custom of honoring elders was not just limited to my own relatives, but to any elderly person who I would meet in public places. For instance, if I would be sitting in a seat on a public bus, I must quickly surrender it to any elderly person who would come close to me on the bus. While I was living in South Korea, even though I was not a Christian, the Korean culture, in my own opinion, was practicing Ephesians 6:2-3 in greater ways than the American culture that has been heavily influenced by the Judeo-Christian ethics: "***Honor your father and mother,*** *" which is the first commandment with promise: that **it may be well with you and you may live long on the earth**.*" After I immigrated to New York City in 1976 during the peak of the Hippy days, I was shocked to discover that the behaviors of (over 90 percent of children who I had encountered in those days) children towards the elderly and their parents were very poor mannered and, in many cases, disrespectful.

The same dishonoring spirits toward parents and elderlies were portrayed in many TV shows and movies as well. The Hollywood movies would frequently depict teenagers and young people as being very disrespectful to their parents and grandparents and showing vulgar and rude manners. They were promoting undisciplined and dishonoring behaviors of children toward their parents as the normal and acceptable culture of society. I do not believe that it was not totally the American children's fault, however, because they were not properly trained like I was trained in Korea: to have respect and a culture of honor for elderly people by my parents and society.

I am not saying that Korean culture was and is better than the American culture, but I can make a generalized statement that, as far as the principle of honoring parents is concerned, Asian culture is definitely better than the Western culture and follows more closely to the Biblical cultural standard. Having said that, I also must declare that there are numerous wonderful cultural standards in the U.S. that are more exemplary than many other cultures in Asia and Korea.

Where Eagles Fly!

I also witnessed that many good American parents were so protective of their children in such a way that it almost appeared to my Korean eyes that they were putting the needs of children above everything else as though they were idols in their lives. Those parents were, in many ways, following the new cultural norm of honoring children more than training them to honor parents, grandparents, and the elderly.

When I heard for the first time that many American parents nicknaming their son as "Buddy", it really confused me and made me wonder why they would want to call their own son a buddy (a companion, partner, and close friend). I was also thinking during my early days in America that such a practice might have been encouraging children to consider their parents as close buddies without being asked to render full respect for them.

Also, I met an elderly gentleman who was 75 years old, so I addressed him as "Sir" or "Mr." by naturally showing my Korean cultural respect. But to my big surprise, he asked me to call him by his first name. In Korea, I would never call any older men or women by their first names. If I did, it would be a great insult to an elderly man or woman. I believe that American cultural norm of calling elderly people by their first names or calling sons as "buddies" has the good intention of narrowing the generational gap by becoming more like friends.

However, the same cultural practice may have contributed in creating a world view for children to emulate less respect or honor for parents and the elderly in general. Another disturbing trend of the relationships between middle upper-class parents and children that I witnessed in those days were that, even though grownup children had already graduated from their universities and had very well-paid jobs, they normally expected parents to initiate telephone calls to check on them and to take care of them, or ignore parents by not contacting them with the excuses of being busy with their lives. When grown-up children who went out for dinner with their parents, they would either split the bill with them or assume the parents would pay the bill and I seldom saw that children would offer to pay the bill. Of course, not all the grownup children behaved like that in America, but I witnessed the majority of them were treating their parents without honor. Also, I can testify that some rich parents' choice for raising their children was to take care of them at all costs without training children to honor the parents or expecting any return from them.

    It appeared to me that rich parents sent their children to elite universities to be successful in life and their successes were credited to the parents' glory. However, as the parents treated their grownup children as though they were still their little babies, I saw the parents controlling their children's affairs and lives and provoking them to anger. Regardless of the situation, I witnessed many children take maximum advantage over their elderly parents or demonstrated the minimum respect and honor for them. My observations on this issue are based on my numerous counseling experiences with those parents who had been disappointed with their children.

    I would advise brokenhearted parents not to have unnecessarily high expectations from their children, but to do their very best to simply love them in the Lord. Conversely, when I was growing up in Korea (unfortunately, I heard that the new young generation of Korean children honor their parents much less than in the 1960's and 1970's of Korea as well), once children graduated from colleges and found good jobs, children would give their first full paycheck to the parents by showing their appreciation of raising them sacrificially. Once the children had secure jobs, they would insist to pay for the bill whenever they went out for lunch or dinner with their parents. Often, I would witness children would fight over the bill if the parents would try to pay. Also, when the parents turned over 60 years old or retired or one of the parents passed away or they became ill, the oldest son or the wealthiest child would take them either into his or her house to take care of them or provide all their needs in their own places until their death. The culture of honor in Korea would require the children to call parents frequently to check on their wellbeing and to take care of their parents and grandparents once they became adults.

Average Korean parents would totally sacrifice themselves to support their children to have master's degrees or even doctoral degrees so they could be successful in their lives. However, once their children reached the place of self-sufficiency, they began to take care of their parents with great respect and honor. Of course, there are plenty of American parents who would totally sacrifice their lives for the sake of their children's success and many godly children take great care of their elderly parents with honor as well.

Another tragedy I have witnessed in America was the fact that many children were left neglected and abused without experiencing any love or care from their parents. Parents' divorces, or unwed single mothers surrendering their children for adoptions, parents bound by drugs, alcohol, sex, gambling addictions, and incarcerated parents relying on the foster care system has resulted in serious social problems in the U.S.

When I counseled many of the child victims of the above, they would express anger, unforgiveness, hatred, bitterness, critical spirits, frustration, and dishonor toward their mothers, fathers, stepparents, and grandparents. I counseled many of the broken and wounded children who tried to commit suicide because of their despair, abandonment, low self-esteem, self-hate, self-condemnation, hopelessness, etc. These children have very legitimate reasons to hate and disrespect their parents because of the abuse that they have received from them in the past. However, I was also able to identify a pattern with those suicidal children. The devil tried to kill those children before their God appointed time because they broke one of the Ten Commandments of God with promise: "*Honor your father and your mother, that your days may be long upon the land which the Lord God is giving you.*"

When I counseled these suicidal children, I would ask them to forgive their parents, stepparents, or adopted parents and try to honor them as best as they could. When they forgave their parents unconditionally, they were freed from the curses of the spirit of suicide. The Bible does not instruct us to honor our father and mother only when they are good and godly parents, but God demands us to honor them regardless of their spiritual conditions or treatment toward us, because we would not be on the earth without them. When we do our very best to honor our parents, then we will have **a long and blessed life on the earth according to God's promise.**

Lastly, I would like to share my personal observations about the sons and daughters-in-law's relationship with fathers and mothers-in-law in America. I was very surprised to witness that many sons and daughters-in-law would call their fathers and mothers-in-law by their first names. That would be an abomination in Korean culture. I believe that once again this cultural practice is an American way of becoming closer to their sons and daughters-in-law like friends to enable their relationship to be smooth and relatable, without having a big generational gap, and treating them equally for the common good. Yet I have also witnessed that many sons and daughters-in-law treats their fathers and mothers-in-law with very minimum respect and honor breaking God's commandment in Ephesians 6:1-3. Unfortunately, I have counseled more parents who have been totally disappointed with their daughters-in-law than sons-in-law. Some mothers-in-law confessed to me that they were also disrespectful and even very hateful to their own mothers-in-law in the past, based on poor treatment by them. Consequently, mothers-in-law confessed that they had received even worse treatments from their own daughters-in-law as though they were punished by the devil for not obeying God's golden rules.

The generational curses can be repeated based on the Scripture in Galatians 6:7, *"Do not be deceived, God is not mocked; for whatever a man sows, that he will also reap."* I once counseled a lady who hated her father and mother-in-law with all her soul and heart because they were very mean to her. She told me that she could hardly endure their presence for an hour when they visited her home. Her mother-in-law was limping in her right leg due to an injury that she had with a car accident. She would despise her mother-in-law's limping leg in her heart whenever she saw her. One day, the daughter-in-law also had a car accident, and her right leg was severely damaged, and she began to limp as well.

When I was counseling her, she confessed to me that she believed that she was punished by God with the same limping in her right leg because she constantly made fun of her mother-in-law's limping leg. Whatever you sow in life, you shall reap according to Galatians 6:7. Therefore, my advice to any son or daughter is that what you do not wish for your future sons and daughters-in-law to do toward you, you must not do currently to your own fathers and mothers-in-law. Also, Jesus Christ's teaching in Matthew 7:1-2 reaffirms the same principle, *"Judge not, that you be not judged. For with what judgment you judge, you will be judged; and with the measure you use, it will be measured back to you."*

FOLLOWING THE CULTURE OF HONOR

Now, let's talk about the Biblical principle on this issue: the Bible never teaches that, *"Parents, honor your sons and daughters so you may live long on the earth."* But it teaches the parents not to provoke them to wrath in Ephesians 6:4, *"And you, fathers, do not provoke your children to wrath, but bring them up in the training and admonition of the Lord."*

Of course, I am generalizing the issue based on how I perceived those parents in America that have chosen to spoil their children and cause them not to honor the elderly. So, I must qualify that I also have witnessed many good and godly American parents teaching their children to respect and honor their parents, grandparents, and the elderly in accordance with the Biblical principles.

It was great to witness that many godly parents showed their deep love and affection for their children, and at the same time, they were training them to follow the Biblically correct ways to respect and honor their parents. In this respect, I loved the godly Christian culture of America much better than the Korean culture. Korean parents taught their children honor and respect for elderlies but did not demonstrate their own deep tangible love and affection for their own sons and daughters.

Due to the belief system of Confucianism that taught parents not to show excessive affection to their own children so that they would not become spoiled, proud, and undisciplined, Korean parents generally showed very limited love for their children in action. When the children did very well, Korean parents hardly praised them. However, when children did anything wrong, they were severely chastised and even ridiculed before their other siblings. I believe that many abused Korean children before the 1970's did not have enough self-confidence in life to be successful due to the negative cultural reinforcement by their parents without receiving any tangible love from them. Since the 1970's Christian revival in Korea, Korean parents began to embrace the Biblical principle of honoring parents and loving their children based on God's mercy, grace, and unconditional love. By the grace of God, the culture of South Korea, which was heavily based on Buddhism and Confucianism, has gradually transformed into following more of God's kingdom culture.

Average South Koreans consider the United States of America as their closest ally and a friendly country because the first group of evangelical missionaries to Korea came from America and they evangelized the Koreans. Additionally, American soldiers fought against Communist North Korea during the Korean War which liberated South Korea to become a democratic and prosperous country. The older South Korean generation would attribute that God's divine mercy and grace caused the American missionaries to introduce Kingdom culture to Korea as well as sending American soldiers to protect South Korea from the evil Communist regime of North Korea. Therefore, I and millions of other Koreans are forever grateful to the Lord for what America has done for South Korea.

REJECTED BY HIS OWN SON

Now let me give you my personal experiences of witnessing several cases of how the disrespecting culture of honor for parents and grandparents has brought great disappointments to multitudes of elderly parents in America. I knew a 75-year-old American man whose wife had passed away several years before I met him (I will call him, Tom). Tom was staying at an apartment with two other elderly men.

Where Eagles Fly!

He became sick and spent all his money for the treatment, so he was just surviving on his meager social security check each month. Tom's only son was a very successful medical doctor who practically abandoned him. Tom told me that he and his wife loved his only son very much and supported and provided for him to graduate from a renown medical school with their middle lower income status.

He told me that he and his wife spoiled their only son very much, and constantly went out of their way to bless and meet many demands of their son. After his son got a very secure position at a large hospital, he would hardly call his parents because he was very busy with his job and his girlfriend. When his son got married, Tom and his wife once again did their very best to help and pay for their part of the cost of his son's wedding. After Tom's son got married, he moved out of his apartment and bought a nice house. Tom's son and his wife would rarely call to see how the parents were doing.

When Tom would ask his son why he was not calling him and his mother from time to time, his answer was that it is the parents' responsibility to check on their son's family and not the children's. When his mother was very sick with cancer, Tom asked his son to help his mother's financial need, and come and visit her often before she would pass away. Unfortunately, his son, who despised his own mother, came to visit her only few times and never financially helped her during her struggle with cancer.

Since Tom had been sick with diabetes and a heart condition, he also asked his son to help him medically and financially, but his son changed his cell phone number and never contacted him again for more than five years. Tom was very disappointed with his son because of his own high expectations of his son to honor and respect him as father was not only disregarded, but he was also abandoned as father.

Where Eagles Fly!

Tom told me that he did not consider him to be his son anymore, showing great sadness in his eyes. He was very bitter toward his son. Tom told me that, probably, his son would not even come for his funeral. I had a chance to share the gospel of Jesus Christ with Tom and prayed for him. I suggested Tom forgive his son and daughter-in-law and try to live with an expectation-free lifestyle in Christ. Tom answered that he had nothing to expect from his son and would try very hard to forgive him.

I have met many American parents who are disappointed with their children who have chosen to dishonor them over the years. The greater the level of expectation from someone who you cared for will create the deeper disappointment in your heart when they do not meet your anticipated return of respect and honor in due seasons of life. We need to accept the reality of the current situation with our loved ones who have been disrespectful toward us. We must turn them over to the Lord so He can deal with them according to His wisdom and power, and forgive them unconditionally.

Unforgiveness toward them will only cause the parents not to be blessed by God according to Matthew 6:14-15. Once we totally forgive them and do not expect anything from them, then we can live the expectation free lifestyle for God's glory and be able to fulfill Luke 6:28, 35 in our lives with God's peace in our hearts:

"Bless those who curse you, and pray for those who spitefully use you. But love your enemies, do good, and lend, hoping for nothing in return; and your reward will be great, and you will be sons of the Most High. For He is kind to the unthankful and evil."

AN ABANDONED PARENT

I knew parents who raised their only son by working very hard at retail stores to provide for all his needs. They had the son in their late 40's, so he was the love of their lives. Unfortunately, they spoiled him all his life and he did not learn to honor or respect his own parents. I will call their names Peter (father), Nancy (mother), and Sam (son). I will describe as best as I can to recall what Peter told me about his situation when I met him. Sam was not a good student and he barely graduated from college.

He began to work odd jobs to provide for himself while he was living at his parent's home. Sam was not a sociable man and he had only a few friends and never dated any girls because he felt he was not an attractive man. Peter and Nancy were Christians, while Sam attended his parent's church when he was a young boy, however he never committed his life to Christ. As he became a teenager, he began to drink alcoholic beverages, take drugs, and fell deep into a sinful lifestyle.

No matter how hard Peter and Nancy prayed for Sam to be changed, he became even more disrespectful to them as he grew older. When Sam was around 42 years old, he finally met a girl (I will call her Julie) whom he eventually married a few years later after living together for a while. Peter and Nancy were very happy that Sam was finally married and had settled down with his wife. However, Sam's wife deeply despised his parents because she was not a Christian and they were constantly asking Sam and Julie to attend church together. Within two years after Sam had married, Julie had a son, and the grandson became the love of Peter and Nancy's life. Unfortunately, shortly after Sam got a new job in a big city seven hours away by car, he moved away from his parents. Eventually, Peter retired from his job and Nancy began to develop minor dementia symptoms. One day, Sam came down to see his parents and suggested that they should sell their house and move up to where they lived so Sam and Julie could take care of them and they could spend more time with their grandson.

Peter and Nancy took Sam's advice, and they sold the house and moved into Sam's home temporarily until they could find another home to live. Within a few weeks of them living with Sam and Julie, Sam stole all his parents' money and put his mother into a nursing home, conspiring together with Julie while Peter was away. When Peter found out about what Sam and Julie did to Nancy without letting him know of their intention, he became furious with them.

Peter went to a police station to ask them to intervene with his situation and ask them to take Nancy out of the nursing home. However, they would not get involved with Peter's domestic situation without having a proper legal litigation against Sam and Julie. Sam even took away Peter's credit cards and kicked him out of his house.

In the meantime, Sam hired a lawyer and made all false charges against his own father and even accused him of also having dementia symptoms so that the social case workers and police would not believe what Peter was testifying against Sam. Peter was broken-hearted when he was not able to take Nancy out of the nursing home to take care of her. In the meantime, Sam made himself guardian over Nancy by making false statements that his father was unreliable to take care of her due to his own dementia problem and had no home to take care of her. When I met Peter, he was a deeply wounded and broken man who even blamed God for allowing his son's deception to destroy their lives. I could not believe my own ears when I heard Peter's story. How could his own son betray his father and mother and abandon them with deception, lies, and manipulation? Peter and Nancy's great disappointment was based on their high expectation of their only son and daughter-in-law to honor and respect them as their parents. I still communicate with Peter from time to time and pray for him. He is now over 80 years old, and Sam never contacted him again after he threw him out of his house and Nancy remains in the nursing home with an advanced dementia and sadly not recognizing Peter at all for many years.

It has been very difficult for me to minister to Peter because he has been very bitter toward Sam and Julie and toward God as well. I tried my very best to ask Peter to forgive Sam and Julie and leave them in the Lord's hand according to His promises in Romans 12:19, *"Beloved, do not avenge yourselves, but rather give place to wrath; for it is written, 'Vengeance is Mine, I will repay,' says the Lord.'"* I prayed with Peter to recommit his life to Christ with all his heart. Peter's great disappointment is based on his high expectation of Sam whom he loved very much as his only son. Sadly, Nancy went to be with the Lord in 2022 and Peter in 2023 with broken-hearts. Sam never went to see them before they passed away.

AN ABANDONED DAUGHTER'S CRY

Margarita and I knew of a lady (I will call her Heather) whose mother was divorced when Heather was two years old, and her father never came to visit her whole life. When she was around 40 years old, she decided to look for her father. After a long search for him, she found out where he was living and got his contact information. She was able to meet with her father and his family for the first time when she was 43 years old. At first, her father and his family

embraced Heather cordially. She was able to forgive her father for abandoning her for over 38 years. They finally reconciled and started a brand-new relationship together as father and daughter. Heather was very happy to get to know her birth father, his wife, half-sisters, and a half-brother.

However, as the father began to spend more time with Heather to catch up with the lost years, jealousies from his wife and daughters began to manifest against her when she visited them. His wife and daughters began to demand that he would choose either his own family or Heather, but he could not have both. It was a heart-breaking decision that the father had to make. Eventually, the father had to declare to Heather that he and his family would not only not allow her to visit them anymore but also, he would not be able to see her again. That news tore Heather's heart apart and almost destroyed her.

She began to question God why He allowed her to find her father and his family to be rejected again by them. She cried out to God that it would have been better if she never found her father again because her pain of the second rejection was much greater than the first abandonment by him. She began to drink again and walked away from God and left the church for several years. She even became suicidal for a while because what she received from her birth father and from God was not what she dreamed and hoped for.

By the time when she found her birth father, she had already been divorced twice with no children. She began to fall deep into the downward spiral of depression, self-hate, self-pity, self-condemnation, unforgiveness, bitterness, anger, and eating disorders. When my wife and I met her, we had to deliver her from the curses of the spirits of rejection, fear, judgement, condemnation, critical and negative attitude, unforgiveness, bitterness, anger, addiction, and loneliness in the name of Jesus Christ. Finally, when she was freed from many demonic spirits that had controlled her for a long time, she asked us to teach her how to live in God's victory each day. We told her that she had to be baptized in the Holy Spirit in order to live a victorious Christian life. When we prayed for her to be filled with the Holy Spirit, she was marvelously baptized in Him and totally set free from all her bondages.

We told her that she needed to rededicate her life to the Lord, join a Spirit-filled church, read the Bible, and pray over everything in life. We also advised Heather to accept her life as it was without having unnecessary high expectations from anyone else and of herself. We encouraged her to live an expectation-free lifestyle by only trusting the Lord with all her heart. Currently, by the grace of God, Heather is living a victorious life in Christ as an eagle Christian for His glory.

HOW TO LIVE EXPECTATION FREE LIFESTYLE

We can only trust God for our lives by hearing the guidance of the Holy Spirit each day. Because Jesus said in John 16:13-15, *"However, when He,* **the Spirit of truth***, has come,* **He will guide you into all truth***; for He will not speak on His own authority, but* **whatever He hears He will speak***; and* **He will tell you things to come***. He will glorify Me, for* **He will take of what is Mine and declare it to you***. All things that the Father has are Mine. Therefore, I said that He will take of Mine and declare it to you."*

In these Scriptures, Jesus declares clearly that the Holy Spirit is the Spirit of truth. That means whatever you hear from the Holy Spirit will be the absolute truth from the Father and Jesus Christ about you, your life, your creation mandate, and your future. Also, Jesus Christ said that the Holy Spirit will guide you into all truth, He will speak to you whatever he hears (from the Father and Jesus Christ), He will tell you things to come, and He will declare what is of Christ to you. Therefore, we need to have a very close communion with the Holy Spirit so that we can be totally guided by God's expectation for our lives each day.

In order for us to be totally guided by the Holy Spirit, we must start with total submission to Him. A yielded life is one God can mold and shape into a vessel of honor for His glory. Submission to the Spirit will enable us to be transformed by His power and wisdom. Every experience of life can be surrendered to His care. God can use every situation, even those from sin or the devil, for His divine purpose in us. God sees the big picture of our trials, and tribulations. He sees the overall picture of our calling, plan, and destiny and the context of the world's needs and individual people's needs. The Holy Spirit sees us from an eternal perspective. Everything is evaluated with His eternal values.[6]

Therefore, we must not put our complete trust or expectation on what loved ones, friends, or people have promised to us because we will be very disappointed if their promises do not come to pass the way we expected. Even Jesus Christ declared that He would not trust men because He knew what was in each person's heart in John 2:23-25, *"Because of the miraculous signs Jesus did in Jerusalem at the Passover celebration, many began to trust in him.* **But Jesus didn't trust them, because he knew all about people. No one needed to tell him about human nature, for he knew what was in each person's heart** *(NLT)."* That means Jesus Christ did not put His trust or expectation on men except for what He received from the Father about them. Therefore, we must put our total trust in the Lord according to Proverb 3:5-6, *"Trust in the Lord with all your heart; and* **lean not on your own understanding**;

in all your ways acknowledge Him, and He shall direct your paths." When we trust the Lord in prayer, we must not demand God to answer our prayers as we expect or desire according to our own understanding, but we must surrender our will to the Lord and expect only His will to be done in our lives according to His own divine purpose and plan.

And should our prayers not be answered according to our own expectations, we must not be discouraged or question God about the outcome. We must accept His will for that matter and thank the Lord for choosing to answer our prayers according to His perfect will regardless of our lack of understanding about the outcome. We must not listen to the lies of the devil; such notions as God does not love us, He does not care about our prayers, He will not answer our prayers because we do not please Him, He wants to take away what we need the most in life, He is punishing us because of our failures, etc. Instead of complaining about God's answer to our prayers that did not materialize according to our desire, we need to trust His judgment based on His promises in Romans 8:35, 37-39:

> *"Can anything ever separate us from Christ's love?* ***Does it mean he no longer loves us if we have trouble or calamity, or are persecuted, or hungry, or destitute, or in danger, or threatened with death?*** *No, despite all these things, over-whelming victory is ours through Christ, who loved us. And* ***I am convinced that nothing can ever separate us from God's love****. Neither death nor life, neither angels nor demons, neither our fears for today nor our worries about tomorrow—not even the powers of hell can separate us from God's love. No power in the sky above or in the earth below—indeed, nothing in all*

creation will ever be able to separate us from the love of God that is revealed in Christ Jesus our Lord." (NLT)

As we put our total expectation on God's perfect will and answer for our lives, our faith will never be altered regardless of so-called negative outcomes. We must respond like Job did after losing everyone and everything that he treasured in Job 2:20-21,

> "Then **Job arose**, tore his robe, and shaved his head; and **he fell to the ground and worshipped**. And he said, 'Naked I came from my mother's womb, and naked shall I return there. The Lord gave, and the Lord has taken away; **blessed be the name of the Lord.**' In all this Job did not sin nor charge God with wrong."

We also need to worship the Lord and bless His name regardless of His answer to our prayers that may be completely unexpected and undesired. As we follow Job's example after facing one of the greatest tragedies in life, the devil will lose his ground over our lives. Where there is worship and praising unto the Lord, the devil will have no power over our lives even though our prayers have not been answered according to our desired expectations.

When we face great disappointment from our parents, children, grandchildren, spouse, siblings, in-laws, friends, leaders of a church, business partners, and co-workers because they failed to meet our expectations, we need to forgive them and turn our unfulfilled prospects over to the Lord. We need to ask the Lord Jesus Christ to take away our discouragements and empower us to live an expectation-free lifestyle. Don Gossett describes in his book, *Praise Avenue*, "*I am convinced that one of the most priceless possessions of the people on Praise Avenue is the power to forgive. You can't buy this power with any amount of money, but it's yours for the asking when you learn to praise God for people who've offended you. Unforgiveness is like a cancer. It starts out as a small speck within us; but if allowed to grow, it will end up as a large, ugly tumor that all but stops our spiritual growth."*[7]

You may still struggle to forgive them because you have been hurt by them so many times in the past and you still must deal with those who have not shown any remorse or changed their attitudes toward you. I would like to suggest you apply Mother Teresa's advice for living a good life:

- *People are often unreasonable, illogical, and self-centered;* **Forgive them anyway.**
- *If you are kind, people may accuse you of selfish, ulterior motives;* **Be kind anyway.**
- *If you are successful, you will win some false friends and some true enemies;* **Succeed anyway.**
- *If you are honest and frank, people may cheat you;* **Be honest and frank anyway.**
- *What you spend years building, someone could destroy overnight;* **Build anyway.**
- *If you find serenity and happiness, they may be jealous;* **Be happy anyway.**
- *The good you do today, people will often forget tomorrow;* **Do good anyway.**
- *Give the world the best you have, and it may never be enough;* **Give the world the best you've got anyway.**
- *You see, in the final analysis, it is between you and God;* **It was never between you and them anyway.**

Where Eagles Fly!

    As you follow the principle of the Beatitudes in Matthew 5:1-12 and Mother Teresa's above advice into your life, you will be able to forgive those who have hurt and disappointed you with God's love. The Greek word *apheimi* [forgive] is used roughly 150 times in the Bible. As is usually the case, the single Greek word offers an anatomy of the notion: **to send away**, to send forth, **to let go**, let be, to permit, allow, not to hinder, to leave, go away from one, to divorce, to leave so that what is left may remain (Thayer & Smith, 1999).

    As you **send** (forgive) those people who had hurt you **away** to Jesus Christ on the cross, He will deal with them with His righteous judgment, so you will be free from any unforgiveness or bitterness toward them. Then you will become God's true eagle Christian to soar up higher than any disappointments, condemnation, anger, discouragements, unforgiveness, bitterness, judgement, or critical spirits to where true eagle Christians fly for God's glory.

Chapter 3

SHAKE OFF THE VIPER

Often times in life, God allows us to go through difficult trials. When we go through the challenging seasons, we must not focus on the evil plans the devil is trying to bring against us, but rather fix our eyes on the Lord to see what He will bring out of even the worst circumstances for His glory. God promised the Israelites that He would be with them when they go through various tribulations in life as described in Isaiah 43:1-3, "*But now, thus says the Lord, who created you, O Jacob, and He who formed you, O Israel: '**Fear not, for I have redeemed you; I have called you by your name; you are Mine**. When you **pass through the waters**, I will be with you; and **through the rivers**, they shall not overflow you. When you walk **through the fire**, you shall not be burned, nor shall the flame scorch you. For I am the Lord your God, the Holy One of Israel, your Savior.'"*

The same promises are applicable to His spiritual Israelites in the New Testament era. In this chapter, we learn from God's mysterious ways how He glorified Himself through Apostle Paul's tribulations on his way to Rome. Prior to the journey, Paul was falsely accused by multitudes of religious Jews and appeared before the Sanhedrin, the high court of justice and the supreme tribunal of the Jews, in Acts 22:30. During the course of Paul's trial before the Jewish religious leaders, the Lord appeared to Paul and said in Acts 23:11, "*Be of good cheer, Paul; **for as you have testified for Me in Jerusalem, so***

you must also bear witness at Rome." From this point on, Paul was assured in his heart that his final mission for Christ would be in Rome—his final destination. When the high priest and the chief men of the Jews petitioned Festus to summon Paul to Jerusalem while there was a plot to kill him on the way (Acts 25:1-3), Paul appealed to Caesar in Acts 25:11, *"For if I am an offender, or have committed anything deserving of death, I do not object to dying; but if there is nothing in these things of which these men accuse me, no one can deliver me to them. I appeal to Caesar.*"

The Lord commissioned Paul with His prophetic mission to Rome; however, in order for the prophecy to be fulfilled in him, Paul had to find the perfect *Kairos* (God ordained time) to declare that he was appealing to Caesar. Thus, Paul's voyage to Rome began in Acts 27 according to God's perfect will. However, I am sure of the fact that Satan did not want Paul to witness for Jesus Christ in Rome, so he began immediately to hinder his journey.

Paul forewarned the crew of the ship that the voyage would end with disaster and much loss, not only of the cargo and ship, but also possibly their lives (Acts 27:10). Nevertheless, the centurion was more persuaded by the helmsman and the owner of the ship than by the things spoken by Paul and proceeded directly into the tempest. Once again, Satan threw his wicked obstacles before Paul's God ordained journey to Rome.

It is obvious that Satan will do everything possible to hinder a chosen man of God from reaching his own destiny, in this case to proclaim the gospel of Jesus Christ in Rome. In the same manner, the devil will do everything possible to hinder you not to reach your God ordained destiny in life. When this happens, you need to be strong in the Lord and very courageous in faith to stand firm on the promises of God and move forward with the authority of Christ and power of the Holy Spirit to conquer your promised land for His glory.

PAUL'S CONSTANT FELLOWSHIP WITH GOD

However, in the midst of the tempest, Paul was in constant fellowship with the Lord and received His assurance of the call to Rome in Acts 27:22-24:

> "*And now I urge you to take heart, for there will be no loss of life among you, but only the ship. For there stood by me this night an angel of God to whom I belong and whom I serve, saying, '**Do not be afraid, Paul; you must be brought before Caesar**; and indeed, God has granted you all those who sail with you.'*"

It is easy for many of us to complain before God when we face such a trial by saying, "*You have called me to go to Rome. Why are you allowing all these trials and tribulations to come to my way? Do You not care about me anymore? If you really love me, deliver me from this tempest and save me.*" Instead of being fearful and complaining before God when we experience the attacks of the devil in our lives, we need to rely completely on Him each step of the way.

If you know for sure that God has been calling you to take your spiritual journey to Rome, then you must totally trust in Him on the way to your final destiny, regardless of what Satan might try to do to hinder you from fulfilling His mission in your life. How often has Satan hindered us when we have engaged in doing God's work. In fact, we should never expect a success unless we hear the devil making a noise.[8] We can learn from how Paul dealt with his own experience with the very deadly storm of his life while he was on God's mission to Rome. Obviously, Paul was in constant prayer before the Lord to know His perfect will for him in the middle of the tempest, just before the shipwreck. Paul was not concerned about his own life because he knew for sure that God would lead him to his final destination to Rome no matter what the devil was doing to derail his mission. And we can see how Paul was more concerned about the others on the ship than himself in Acts 27:33b-36:

> *"Today is the fourteenth day you have waited and continued without food and eaten nothing. Therefore,* ***I urge you to take nourishment, for this is for your survival, since not a hair will fall from the head of any of you.*** *And when he had said these things, he took bread and gave thanks to God in the presence of them all; and when he had broken it, he began to eat. Then they were all encouraged, and also took food themselves."*

Regardless of being in the midst of a very difficult circumstance, Paul gave thanks to God in their presence and encouraged them to take nourishment. We too should follow Paul's example, giving thanks to the Lord in the middle of our own trials and tribulations and not focusing on the devil but trusting in the Lord with all our hearts. When we focus on Satan, he will release spirits of fear to bind us and guide us to lose focus on God and His promises and purposes. Therefore, as we go through fire like trials in life, we must not focus on the fire but God who walks with us through the fire. Then we will come out of our trials victoriously and God will use them for His glory.

PAUL WAS BITTEN BY A VIPER

The sailors ran the ship aground on the shore of the island of Malta and all the people in the ship including Paul were able to escape safely. On Malta, Acts 28:2-3 states, *"The natives showed them unusual kindness; for they kindled a fire and made them all welcome, because of the rain that was falling and because of the cold. But when Paul had gathered a bundle of sticks and laid them on the fire****, a viper came out because of the heat, and fastened on his hand****."*

Now Paul just escaped the shipwreck and he wanted to warm himself up around the fire. But the devil did not want him to go to Rome to be the witness of Jesus Christ, so he tried to kill Paul with the venom of the viper in Malta. However, Paul who was assured of his final destiny by the Lord was calm and didn't react to the potential life-threatening danger of being bitten by a viper. He knew that he was not going to die in Malta but would go to the God-ordained city of Rome to declare the Kingdom of God, and eventually die there.

We can learn from Paul when we face a life-threatening situation: we must be calm, and neither be fearful of the venom of a viper nor be focused on the potential effects of it. The more we focus our attention on the viper's venom, the greater the spirit of fear that will be released to paralyze our minds and hearts so we will not be able to reach our spiritual destiny. When the enemy's viper bites us, we immediately need to put our total trust in the Lord and His promises.

Now let's continue with the story of Paul in Acts 28:4-6, *"So when the natives saw the creature hanging from his hand, they said to one another, 'No doubt this man is a murderer, whom, though he has escaped the sea, yet justice does not allow to live.' But **he shook off the creature into the fire and suffered no harm**. However, they were expecting that he* *would swell up or suddenly fall down dead. But after they had looked for a long time and saw no harm come to him, they changed their minds and said that he was a god."*

Like Paul, we need to shake off the viper into God's fire and allow His divine peace to guard our hearts and minds in Christ Jesus until we experience His total victory and peace over that matter. There is only one person that we can totally commit ourselves to, to whom we can turn over our family, our lives, our possessions, our mind, our spirit, our bodies, everything. That one person is Jesus Christ. And that is what it means to be a Christian—to totally commit ourselves to Jesus as our Lord, as our only God.[9]

Notice that when a terrible thing happens to a person, often the people around him gossip about him among themselves, rendering the judgment that he might have sinned before God, or he deserves to receive God's punishment due to his hidden sins. Then they will monitor his fate to be decided based on the outcome of the viper's attack. In Paul's case, as the inhabitants of Malta waited to see what would happen to him, he shook off the viper into the fire and suffered no harm. Then the spectators changed their minds and considered him as a god.

Now, God was about to use what the devil meant for evil for His own good. In life, God may allow you to be bitten by a viper so that He can use that occasion to bless someone else. Let's examine how God used the viper's attack against Paul to bring Hid divine healing to all those who were sick in Acts 28:7-9:

> *"In that region there was an estate of the leading citizen of the island, whose name was Publius, who received us and entertained us courteously for three days. And it happened that the father of Publius lay*

sick of a fever and dysentery. **Paul went into him and prayed, and he laid his hands on him and healed him.** *So, when this was done,* **the rest of those on the island who had diseases also came and were healed**."

God used the occasions of Paul's shipwreck by Malta and viper bite to bless the inhabitants. If he was not bitten by the viper, God would not be able to use Paul to heal all who had diseases on the island. God can also use the metaphoric viper bites in our lives for His glory. So, when we are bitten by a viper during the journey of our lives, we must not focus on the viper's venom or the fear factor of what may happen to us, but we must throw it immediately to the fire of the Lord in faith. Then we need to pray and ask the Lord to use the occasion for His glory so that the devil will not have victory over us.

MY PERSONAL EXPERIENCES OF BEING BITTEN BY VIPERS

There have been numerous occasions in my full-time missions work in the nations over the past 37 years where God allowed vipers to bite me so that He could use what the devil meant for evil for His glory. While I was going through the process of dealing with the vipers, it was not easy for me to shake them off into the fire of God quickly. I was frustrated, confused, angry at the devil, complaining before God, and pleading with Him to deliver me whenever I was bitten by a viper during the most unpredictable circumstances.

After experiencing God turn the situation around several times for His glory in my life, I gradually began to trust the Lord and sought His perfect plan, purpose, and will for the occasion when the viper had bitten me. I would like to share three stories of how God used my own viper bite cases for His glory to save someone along the way. A. W. Tozer said in his book *The Knowledge of the Holy*, *"The God of glory sometimes revealed Himself like a sun to warm and bless, indeed, but often to astonish, overwhelm, and blind before He healed and bestowed permanent sight. We have only to prepare Him a habitation in love and faith and humility."*[10]

PAINFUL ABSCESSED TOOTH IN BULGARIA

Once I was conducting a five-day seminar in Plovdiv, Bulgaria and I began to have a severe pain in one of my lower left teeth. It started on the second day of the seminar and the pain in and around the tooth was much worse on the morning of the third day. I knew it was abscessed because of the level of pain that I was experiencing. I began to pray and ask the Lord to take away the pain by His supernatural power because in 1994 I didn't want to go see a Bulgarian dentist. The dental technology in Bulgaria in those days was much more primitive compared to the standard in the U.S.

I sincerely prayed to the Lord to heal me supernaturally every possible moment for two full days. It was so painful that I had a difficult time sleeping. I was reasoning with the Lord that I was doing His will and He needed to heal me for His glory. The harder I prayed for healing the greater pain was manifesting on the abscessed tooth. When I prayed the very first day for my dental issue, the Holy Spirit asked me to go and see a female dentist in town. I kept reasoning with the Lord that I didn't want to see a Bulgarian female dentist because of my fear knowing that the dentistry in Bulgaria was far behind that of the U.S.

I complained before God that He had all power to heal me completely if He would only choose to. I reasoned with God that He needed to heal me so that I didn't have to skip a session to see the dentist. I presumptuously reminded God that He had to follow through with His promises in Matthew 19:29 as I was doing the will of God in Bulgaria:

> *"And everyone who has left houses or brothers or sisters or father or mother, or wife or children or lands, for My name's sake, shall receive a hundredfold, and inherit eternal life."*

Because I left my home, country, wife, and children for His name's sake, I petitioned God to heal me quickly and super-naturally for His glory. However, God did not answer my prayer as I was expecting, and my tooth pain became unbearable on the morning of the third day of the seminar. Finally, I asked my interpreter to search for a female dentist in town for me to see her as quickly as possible. The interpreter told me that there was a very good Christian male dentist who attended the church and the seminar, and she could arrange for him to treat my dental problem as soon as possible.

So, I asked the Lord again if I could see the male dentist in the church. But the Holy Spirit once again answered emphatically that I had to see a female dentist in town. Therefore, I asked the interpreter to find a female dentist in town for me to see that day. She gave me a very puzzled look and asked me why I would want to see an unknown female dentist whom she needed to find, while the church had a very good male Christian dentist who could see me right away. I explained to her that I strongly felt the guidance of the Holy Spirit to see a female dentist in town. She reluctantly told me that she would look into it and let me know. I had to suffer for

Where Eagles Fly!

two more hours with my severe toothache before she came and told me that she found one female dentist in town. However, she informed me that she was also a very well-known atheist during the Communist time, and had persecuted Christians in Plovdiv. She begged me to see the Christian dentist in her church. Once again, I asked the Lord if it would be all right for me to see the Christian male dentist from the church. But His answer—No—was very clear and He commended me to obey His guidance.

Finally, I went to see the female dentist in town. When she saw me, she acted as though she was interrogating me about my dental issues with a very stern Communist face. I told her the whole story of when the pain started and how painful it was for the past three days. She began to poke the gum area of my abscessed tooth and I screamed with pain. She told me that it was abscessed, and she needed to do a root canal. In the U.S. I had to take antibiotic pills to reduce the infection first before any dentist would do a root canal treatment. So, I questioned her, *"Don't you need to give me an antibiotic medication first to get rid of the infection before you do the root canal treatment?"*

She told me that the infection was not so bad, and she could to the root canal treatment right away. She also asked me if I wanted to have a Novocain injection prior to the treatment. I was even shocked to hear that anyone would consider doing a root canal without any Novocain. So, I asked her, *"Is it an option to have a Novocain shot prior to have a root canal treatment in Bulgaria?"* She said, *"Yes, it is an option, and you have to pay 100 Leva per shot. Unfortunately, some poor Bulgarians who cannot afford to pay will do the procedure without the shots."* I told her that I would pay for however many shots she needed to numb my gum prior to the procedure.

Without providing any kind or comforting words prior to the procedure, she gave me two shots to numb my gum and began the root canal in my painful tooth. By the grace of God, the Novocain shots worked, and I did not feel any pain during the procedure. I was still wondering why I had to come and see the atheist female dentist, so I asked the Lord to let me know the purpose of seeing her. The Holy Spirit whispered in my heart that I should pray for her healing in her back after she finished with the root canal treatment.

I was able to notice that she was touching her back a few times while she was performing the root canal procedure on me. However, I was thinking that she would not want me to pray for her if she was an atheist. So, I asked the Lord to give me His divine wisdom for me to talk with her about her back pain issues. Finally, she finished the procedure and told me that the root canal treatment went well, and I should not have any more pain or problem in that tooth. I thanked her and I asked her to hear why I came to see her. I told her the whole story of how the Lord asked me to come and see her instead of the male dentist from the church.

She told me that she did not believe in God, she was an atheist. I gave her the word of knowledge that she had been suffering with back pain for over 10 years and she was thinking about retiring from the dental practice because of it. I told her that it was not a coincidence that I came to see her, but it was God's divine appointment. I said to her, "*What will be the chance that she will treat a Korean-American evangelist who happens to be ministering in her city?*" I told her that I prayed for several people who had been suffering with back pains for some time and they were totally healed during the seminar at the church. So, I challenged her what would she lose if she could be healed when I prayed for her back. The dentist reluctantly allowed me to pray for her back. I asked her permission to put my hand on her back where she felt the most pain. Then, I began to quietly pray for her back to be totally healed by the power of God. As I was praying for a few minutes, she began to express that she felt as though fire was on her back where I placed my hand. Soon, she began to cry softly that she did not feel any pain in her back for the first time in 10 years. I asked her to stand up and move her back to see if there was any more pain. She got up and began to bend her back and touch her toes with her hands, and she had no pain. She, for the first time since my appointment began, smiled and then gave me a big hug.

I told her that God loved her so much that He allowed me to have an abscessed tooth so that I had to come and see her— He told me to come and see a female dentist in Plovdiv. If I did not have the dental issue, I would have never come to see her. She allowed me to share the salvation message of Jesus Christ for over 20 minutes and at the end of my presentation of the gospel, by the grace of God and the power of the Holy Spirit, I was able to lead her to accept Jesus Christ as her Lord and Savior.

I also prayed for her to receive the baptism of the Holy Spirit and she felt the fire of God going through her whole body. She repented of her sins of unbelief and rejection of God. After she became a born-again believer in Christ, I could see the transformation of her face and demeanor. She gave me another big hug and told me that she was so glad that God sent me to see her so she could be healed and saved. I later heard that she joined the church and began to serve the Lord. Praise the Lord! God allowed a viper to bite me during a wonderful seminar in Plovdiv, Bulgaria. Because of the incident, I was sent to the only female dentist in the area, by the direction of the Holy Spirit. God loved her so much that He would allow me to suffer with an abscessed tooth so His salvation and healing could come upon an atheist female dentist. I learned a very important lesson: I must not immediately complain before God whenever unexpected tribulation occurs, because God can use what the devil meant for evil for His own glory to save and heal someone through it. Therefore, I can truly accept the Scriptures in Philippians 2:12b-13, "...*work out your own salvation with fear and trembling;* **for it is God who works in you both to will and to do for His good pleasure**."

What God has been working in our lives whether they seem like good or bad cases, are all for His good pleasure and glory. We must learn to wait upon the Lord before we initiate the course of action for doing His work no matter how difficult and unpleasant it may appear in our own eyes, because it is not for our pleasure but for His own good pleasure. How can we fulfill the call and will of God in our life? By waiting on the Lord...

> "*But those who wait on the Lord Shall renew their strength;* **they shall mount up with wings like eagles**, *they shall run and not be weary, they shall walk and not faint.*" (Isaiah 40:31)

MY FRONT TOP BRIDGE CAME OFF

I was about to go to a church to teach one of the Global Harvest Network (GHN) courses: "*How to move in God's Kingdom Authority and Power*" seminar in St. Petersburg, FL on a Saturday morning for three hours. Suddenly, my top front dental bridge came off and fell out of my mouth for no reason. Prior to that moment, I had some breakfast without feeling any looseness of my bridge. We got some temporary dental adhesive from a local drug store to reglue the bridge back to the front upper part of my implanted teeth, but it wasn't working well. I was praying and asking God to help me to teach with a loose bridge. I also said to the Holy Spirit in my heart, *"What are you doing? Lord! Do you have another divine appointment for me to fulfill today? Please do something to keep the bridge from falling off while I will be teaching because if it happens again, it will be a very embarrassing event for me."* The Lord did not say anything specific about what He was going to do with my problem, but I felt in my spirit He was going to use this event for His glory. Once again, God allowed me to be bitten by a viper (so to speak) so that He could use it to bless someone.

When I arrived at the church, I told the participants of the seminar that my top front bridge had fallen off and I temporarily put it back by using dental adhesive from a local drugstore. I told them not to laugh if it fell off. Meanwhile, I asked the pastor to find out if any dental office in the city would attend to emergency patients on a Saturday, and if he could find one, to make an appointment for me to see a dentist to reattach the bridge. As I was teaching, the bridge almost came off a few times.

By the grace of God, I was able to finish the seminar around 12:30 p.m. and we began to have lunch and fellowship. I couldn't eat anything so I asked the pastor if he was able to locate a dentist. He was smiling at me and told me that he called more than 11 dental offices in town and none of them were opened on Saturday. However, when he contacted the 12th dental office, an assistant told him that they would be open until 2:00 p.m. I quickly made an appointment and went over right away. When I arrived, I was the only patient, so I was escorted to the room by an assistant. She asked me what the problem was, and I told her that my top front upper bridge over my implanted teeth had fallen off for no reason. She told me she was very sorry to hear that. However, when I heard the assistant talking in English, I was able to detect a unique Ukrainian accent. So, I asked her, "Are you from Ukraine?" She said yes. I asked her, "Where are you from in Ukraine?" She told me that she was from Ternopil. After my big surprise, I told her that I had been ministering at Ethnos Church in Ternopil for the past five years. When I told her that, she began to cry and said to me, "I am a Christian and attended Ethnos church in Ternopil before I moved here three years ago." She told me that she was so homesick that morning that she prayed to the Lord to send someone who had been visited Ternopil and known Ethnos church to see her. She was crying and laughing at the same time and told me that God had answered her prayers.

I said to her, "God surely answered your prayers by making my bridge loose so I had to come to see you." I began to show her my Facebook friends from Ethnos church and she excitedly told me that she knew almost all of them. For the next 20 minutes, she was more interested in talking with me about the church and her friends. Finally, the dentist came to attend to my need and re-cemented my fallen bridge. When the dentist found out about her assistant's story, she was amazed by the fact that God's divine care and love for one of His daughters caused me to come and see her.

The assistant gave me a big hug and praised the Lord for answering her prayer before I left the office. I was also rejoicing before God that He used me to encourage a lonely Ukrainian dental assistant when she was so sad and downhearted that day. Once again, God allowed me to go through an ordeal that time so that I could be a blessing to a lonesome young lady from Ukraine. Since then, she has studied and became a dentist. God wants us to soar up high to where eagle Christians fly so we can perceive and fulfill His extended vision that can only be seen on a higher spiritual altitude for our lives. If we allow God to use every trial that we face in life for His glory, then He can use it to bless someone who needs the touch of God's tangible love through us. God has the power to turn what the devil meant for evil for His own good according to His promise in Romans 8:28, *"And we know that **all things work together for good** to those who love God, to those who are the **called according to His purpose.**"* We, as the sons and daughters of God, must do our very best to make all things (including trials, tribulations, sicknesses, and dangers) work together for good according to His divine purpose and plan.

MY T-12 VERTEBRA FRACTURE

I went to conduct the Global Harvest Network (GHN) Conference in north-east India next to Bhutan in March 2018. I went with four other GHN equippers to train over 70 selected indigenous leaders who came from the unreached regions of northern India. I had created the GHN courses to train indigenous leaders to evangelize their own Unreached People Groups (UPGs) in their region. To accomplish that, I first trained American Missions Mobilizers (MMs) through the GHN seminars in the U.S. Then, I took a selected group of them to the nations to equip indigenous MMs.

In turn, trained national MMs can train other indigenous MMs to evangelize their own and other UPGs in adjacent regions. Through implementing the GHN missions strategy, Western missionaries may not be needed to engage in doing the kingdom work in the nations as long-term missionaries. Instead, they can become equippers of indigenous MMs as short term GHN trainers. During the conference, I taught them how to move in God's Kingdom authority and power to evangelize the UPGs in the region by moving in signs, wonders, and miracles. Many of the pastors and leaders expressed that they were truly baptized in the Holy Spirit during the conference, and they learned how to move in God's supernatural authority and power in the name of Jesus Christ to destroy the works of the devil among their own UPGs. I was also able to minister at several different indigenous churches. During this trip, over 30 people claimed that they were supernaturally healed when GHN team prayed for them.

On the morning of March 27, 2018, I went early to the office to create the March River of Life Ministries (RLM) Newsletter. It was around 12:15 p.m., I received a telephone call which distracted me from writing the newsletter and caused me to lose my focus. While I was talking on the phone, the mounted bookshelves above my desk, which weighed at least 300 pounds, suddenly came down, hit my head, and knocked me to the floor. My head was opened and profusely bleeding, the middle of my spinal column was bulged out, and I was in the most excruciating pain I had ever felt in my life.

My assistant came in and was shocked to see me screaming in pain with blood all around me, the room looking as though it was hit by a powerful earthquake. She got a towel and tried to put pressure on my open head injury to stop the bleeding. She pulled me out of the piles of books and bookshelves over my body while I was feeling agonizing pain in my back. She called 911 and the emergency paramedics were on their way and called Margarita to come to the office quickly. Within five minutes, five paramedics were in my office and soon my wife also arrived.

I asked Margarita, my assistant, and the paramedics to pray with me prior to doing anything to check on me. They reluctantly agreed to pray with me. Once they gathered around me, I began to praise and worship the Lord despite what had happened. I asked the Lord to have mercy on me and miraculously heal me in three days. Then they began to check me and covered my head with bandages and gauzes to stop the bleeding. They put me on a stretcher and took me down from the upstairs office very carefully. They put me in an ambulance and drove me to the emergency room of Sentara Princess Anne Hospital in Virginia Beach. I was having intense pain in my back and had to wait for a doctor to come and see me. Then a young female doctor came in, checked my vital signs and asked me several questions relating to the injury. She ordered a CAT scan for my head and an MRI for my spinal cord. By the grace of God, I did not have any concussion or internal bleeding in my head. However, I had a compressed fracture on T-12 vertebra and was bleeding inside of my spinal cord.

There were so many people at the emergency room that I had to wait for more than three hours in the hallway to be admitted into a treatment room. The nurse on duty gave me a strong pain killer but it did not alleviate my pain too much. The doctor put in six staples to close my open wound on the top right-side of my head. She repeated asked me, *"What is your name? Do you know the date? When is your birthday?"* She was checking my cognizant responses after my head injury. She also asked me if I had any headache or pain in my head. It was a miracle that I did not have any serious injuries on my head, and I did not even have a headache.

However, I was having excruciating pain in the center of my back. The nurse gave me another painkiller. I asked her what kind of painkiller it was. She told me that it was an opioid. Opioids are highly addictive substance. I had already taken three opioids for my pain, and if I took more than four of them, I could be on the path to addiction. Therefore, I told her that I did not want to take any more opioids and asked her to give me another kind that was not as an addictive drug.

She gave me very strong Tylenol instead. They kept me overnight in the emergency room and released me at around 3:30 p.m. the next day. Margarita took me to her car in a wheelchair, and it was a great challenge for me to climb up to the passenger seat because of my back pain. After I came home, one of the most difficult things I had to do was to get up out of my bed, hold onto the walker to go to the bathroom. My T-12 vertebra area was swollen and hurting badly. I decided not to take any painkillers and asked the Lord again to heal me completely in three days so I could rise and walk on the fourth day without a walker or crutches.

The Lord assured me that I would be healed on the fourth day. The physician at the emergency room told me that I would have a very difficult time sitting in a chair for a long time or walking for at least three months. However, I told her that I would be healed in three days and walk again on the fourth day without a walker or crutches. When I told her that, she rolled her eyes in unbelief.

I was scheduled to preach to over 200 young people at a local church in Chesapeake, VA on April 13th. I also already booked my flight to Ukraine to minister at three different churches and to conduct the Global Harvest Network (GHN) conference at a Ukraine Missions School near Kiev from April 17th to the 30th. I promised the Lord that I would continuously minister as long as He would heal me and empower me to have His divine life and health.

However, the first three days I experienced unbearable pain to get up and move. I was constantly praying and asking the Lord to heal me in three days and to allow me to preach at the youth revival meeting on the evening of April 13th. I put my total faith in God and His promises in the Bible and not on the negative and depressing words of the physician at the emergency room. The doctor told me that I should cancel all my preaching engagements for at least three months until I would be gradually healed. She also told me that it would be very difficult for me to sit on an economy seat to fly to Ukraine in three weeks due to the T-12 compression fracture. Nevertheless, as I was laying on the bed or couch for three days with great pain, I was constantly picturing myself standing up and preaching to the young people in two weeks and flying to Ukraine to minister at different churches and teaching the GHN courses to Ukrainian young people in three weeks without any pain.

I was trying very hard to put my faith into action by totally trusting and envisioning God's promises in Jeremiah 30:17, *"For I will restore health to you and heal you of your wounds, says the Lord."* I pleaded with the Lord that He would heal me based on His abundant grace and mercy. I promised the Lord that I would also go to Ukraine and other nations to preach the Kingdom of God if He would heal me in these three days.

I also kept praising and even thanking the Lord for the accident, because I absolutely believed that what the devil meant for evil for my life and ministry, God would turn it around for good and for His glory to save, heal, and deliver someone through my testimony of His miracle healing. I also asked the Lord to give me a special healing anointing to heal anyone who would be suffering with any type of back pain. On the morning of the fourth day, I was still feeling great pain in my back, so I got up out of my bed and came out to the living room to lay down on my couch.

I was listening to Christian worship songs and praising the Lord in my heart. Margarita came to me and asked me how I was doing. She took great care for me for three full days without going anywhere. I told her that I was still in pain. She asked me, *"Can I go out to buy some groceries at a local Walmart? I will come back home as quickly as I can"* She was concerned about leaving me at home by myself. I told her that I would be all right. She asked me to call her if I needed her for anything. I told her that I would be alright. As I was laying on my couch, I once again reminded the Lord that it was the fourth day and I needed to be healed so I could walk to the church to praise Him on Resurrection Sunday in two days. I said the Lord, *"If my body is the temple of the Holy Spirit and His temple had the T-12 compression fracture, then it is His responsibility to fix His own damaged temple for His glory."*

    A dreadful moment came upon me that afternoon because I needed to get up and push my body with the walker to go to the bathroom. I slowly got up out of the couch and I realized that I did not feel any sharp pain anymore when I moved my back. I got up gradually and began to take the first step without the walker and I did not feel any pain again. So, I began to walk toward the bathroom by myself without feeling any pain. Then, I came out of the bathroom, and I decided to walk upstairs to test how I would feel. Because the doctor told me that one of the most difficult things for me to do would be to walk up steps.

    Therefore, I decided to slowly walk up the stairs and reached upstairs without any pain. I began to praise the Lord and thank Him for answering my prayers. I ran down the stairs and back upstairs two more times without feeling any pain in my back. When I checked my back around T-12 vertebra, the fractured area that was bulged out was gone and felt normal. I was rejoicing in the Lord and worshipping Him with all my heart. God is faithful and His mercy and grace endures forever. I called Margarita and showed her via "FaceTime" that I was walking upstairs and downstairs without feeling any pain. She was crying and praising the Lord for His miraculous healing upon me.

Where Eagles Fly!

By God's absolute grace and mercy, on Resurrection Sunday, I walked to the church and worshipped the Lord and thanked Him for His divine healing. I was also able to preach at the youth revival meeting two weeks later. Many young people accepted the Lord and almost all of them were touched by the power of the Holy Spirit and fell to the floor during the altar calls. I was ministering to them until 11:30 p.m. that night. Since then, I sometimes feel 3-5% of back pain as if it is a thorn in my flesh. I have been asking the Lord to heal me completely, but His grace has been sufficient for me. Three weeks after the accident, I went to Ukraine to minister for two weeks.

Once again, the Lord moved mightily and saved many young people and healed many people with any type of back pain. Since then, I have ministered in Colombia, Ukraine (five times), Kyrgyzstan, Spain, Singapore, Myanmar, Cuba, Costa Rica, Cambodia, Vietnam, Indonesia, South Korea, Guatemala, Malaysia, Bulgaria, Netherlands, Peru, and Poland for God's missions work for His glory. Regardless of how I felt in my back, I have decided never to give the devil any victory over my life. Jesus Christ has all of me and through the power of the Holy Spirit, I can do all things through Him who strengthens me each day.

Because of my back pain after the accident, my doctor recommended me to have some massage therapy. So, I began to visit a local therapeutic massage therapist from time to time—especially after my long overseas trips. Whenever I would visit a massage therapist, I witnessed to her about Jesus Christ. I was able to lead one therapist (I will call her Helen) to the Lord after the session and prayed for her to be filled with the Holy Spirit. After several months passed, Helen got in touch with me via the ministry website and told me that she was truly born-again and filled with the Holy Spirit when I prayed for her. She felt the fire of the Holy Spirit going through her body and was able to forgive all the people who had hurt her in the past. She was a New Ageist as well as a Satanist. That night, she got rid of her Satanist bible, and many other New Age books and idols which were worth over $1,000. She thanked me for sharing with her about the gospel of Jesus Christ.

I was truly amazed by how God had used me to set a Satanist free from the bondage of darkness. I thanked the Lord for using my back injury to lead a daughter of Satan to be a daughter of the living God. If I did not have the back injury, I would never have had a chance to see a massage therapist. God allowed me to be bitten by a viper, but He used the occasion to not only to lead Helen to the Lord but also to set multitudes of others who were suffering with back pain free in the U.S. and in the nations for His glory.

Whenever I shared my testimony of how God healed me of my severe back injury, I was able to pray for many others who were suffering with various sicknesses and they were healed by the grace of God. If we ever get bitten by a viper, we need to be bold to shake it off into the fire of God and allow Him to use the occasion to save, heal, and deliver someone for His glory. Then we will be God's Eagle Christians to soar up high by the wind of the Holy Spirit to accomplish His divine purpose and will for our lives wherever He sends us to shine His light to the people under the power of darkness.

Chapter 4

ARISE AND SHINE FOR YOUR LIGHT HAS COME

Just like Isaiah prophesied in Isaiah 60:1-2, the darkness will cover the earth, and deep darkness over the people—even the elect:

> *"Arise, shine; for your light has come! And the glory of the Lord is risen upon you. For behold, the darkness shall cover the earth, and deep darkness the people; but the Lord will arise over you, and His glory will be seen upon you."*

As we watch the news each night, we are able to identify many signs of the end times unfolding in front of our eyes since the beginning of the COVID-19 worldwide pandemic. Our Lord Jesus Christ warned the disciples what will take place before the Great Tribulation in Matthew 24:5-14:

> *For many will come in My name, saying, '**I am the Christ,**' **and will deceive many**. And you will hear of **wars and rumors of wars**. See that you are not troubled; for all these things must come to pass, but the end is not yet. **For nation will rise against nation, and kingdom against kingdom. And there will be famines, pestilences, and earthquakes in various***

places. *All these are the beginning of sorrows.* ***Then they will deliver you up to tribulation and kill you, and you will be hated by all nations for My name's sake.*** *And then many will be offended, will betray one another, and will hate one another.* ***Then many false prophets will rise up and deceive many.*** *And because* ***lawlessness will abound***, *the love of many will grow cold. But he who endures to the end shall be saved. And* ***this gospel of the kingdom will be preached in all the world*** *as a witness to all the nations, and* ***then the end will come***.

Let us examine the above prophetic Scriptures carefully:

- **Many will come in My name, I am the Christ and will deceive many:** For the past few decades, many deceiving voices have been preached in the name of Christ to cause great confusion in the Church. Those voices have been released to specialize in their brands of the gospel to build their own religious kingdoms on earth. They seldom proclaim the full spectrum of the gospel in accordance with the principles of the four gospels that were preached and demonstrated by Jesus Christ.

    Also, they do not follow the examples of how the apostles in the book of Acts preached and expanded the Kingdom of God by affirming the work of the Holy Spirit through signs, wonders, and miracles following. They normally specialize in a narrowly focused part of the gospel to gather their followers to build their own kingdom on earth in the name of Christ. Jesus Christ declared in Matthew 28:18, *"All authority has been given to me in heaven and on earth."* Also, He said in Acts 1:8, *"But you shall receive power when the Holy Spirit has come upon you; and you shall be witnesses to Me in Jerusalem, and in all Judea and Samaria, and to the end of the earth."* Furthermore, Jesus Christ very clearly defined His mission on earth in 1 John 3:8b, *"For this purpose the Son of God was manifested, that He might destroy the works of the devil."*

Then, the true ministers of the Kingdom of Heaven must move in the authority of Christ and the power of the Holy Spirit to destroy the works of the devil in their own Jerusalem, Judea, and Samaria. They also must send missions mobilizers to the end of the earth to equip indigenous missionaries to evangelize their own Unreached People Groups (UPGs) with signs, wonders, and miracles following until Jesus Christ comes back.

- **Wars and rumors of wars:** According to the *Infoplease* website article: *"Major military operations since World War II"* describes that there have been 17 different conflicts that the U.S. has directly been involved in with worldwide conflicts. Israel has fought 18 wars with Arabs since the inception of the nation in 1948. On February 24, 2022, Russia invaded Ukraine in a major escalation of the Russo-Ukrainian War, which began in 2014.

  They sent over 20,000 troops, tanks, and other armored vehicles toward Kyiv and to eastern Ukrainian regions, and unfortunately, the war is still going on in Ukraine as of April 2025. Currently, China has been threatening to take over Taiwan militarily.

Tragically, nations will rise against nations and kingdom against kingdom until the day of the Lord's return.[11]

- **Famines, pestilences, and earthquakes in various places:** *The World Counts* declares that around 9 million people die every year of hunger and hunger-related diseases. This is more fatal than other diseases such as: AIDS, malaria, tuberculosis, and the COVID-19 pandemic combined. For the past 100 years, approximately 95 million people have died due to various pestilences.[12] *Our World in Data* describes that natural disasters kill on average 45,000 people per year and are responsible for 0.1% of global deaths.[13]

  Bloomberg CityLab states that between 1900 and 2015, there have been more than 10,000 strong earthquakes, with magnitudes of 6 or greater, around the world.[14] Between 2016 and 2024, there have been 25,784 earthquakes worldwide according to various sources. Bible prophesy on earthquakes has been occurring in throughout the world and it will only intensify as we face the last hour of the Last Days.

- **They will deliver you up to tribulation and kill you:** *Christian Today* states that approximately 70 million Christians have been martyred for their faith since Jesus walked the earth.[15] *Fox News* states that nearly one million Christians have reportedly been martyred for their faith worldwide in the last decade.[16] Unfortunately, there will be many more Christian martyrs throughout the world before the second coming of Christ according to Revelation 6:9-11, *"When He opened the fifth seal, I saw under the* *altar the souls of those who had been slain for the word of God and for the testimony which they held. And they cried with a loud voice, saying, "How long, O Lord, holy and true, until You judge and avenge our blood on those who dwell on the earth?" Then a white robe was given to each of them; and it was said to them that **they should rest a little while longer, until both the number of their fellow servants and their brethren, who would be killed as they were, was completed.***"

- **Many false prophets will rise up and deceive many:** *Watchman Fellowship* states that there are over 1,200 indexes of cults and false religions in the world.[17] Just like the days of Jeremiah, many false prophets have risen to deceive, manipulate, and misguide multitudes of the elect to be led astray from the truth and purpose of the word of God. We, the believers in Christ, must read the whole Bible and stand on the word of God so that we may not be deceived. We must also constantly pray in the Spirit so that He can guide us into all truth according to John 16:13-15.

- **Lawlessness will abound:** We can witness the present state of lawlessness in the U.S. It began gradually moving away from the original Judeo-Christian values by taking God, the Bible, and prayer out of our public-school system in 1963. They have replaced the godly principles of the Bible with secular humanistic books that contradict the truth of the Bible. As a result, the nation has been embracing socialistic ideas to destroy biblical values at all levels of society.

World Atlas declares that the 2000s was the decade with the highest number of crimes, with 115.2 million reported crimes in the U.S.[18] For the past 20 years, there have been numerous riots, murders, crimes, and violent mass shootings throughout cities in the U.S. and the trend has been getting worse since millions of illegal migrants have been flooding into our Southern border.

- **This gospel of the kingdom will be preached in all the world:** Jesus Christ declared that this gospel of the kingdom will be preached in all the world as a witness [*marturion* in Greek: testimony] to all the nations [*ethnos*: ethnic groups, people groups], and then the end [*telos*: finished, fulfillment, ends] will come. The most current *Joshua Project* states that there are 17,280 total people groups in the world and 4,422 Frontier People Groups [*ethnos*] are considered as the least Unreached People Groups.[19]

    The gospel of the kingdom will be preached to all 4,422 people groups in the near future in order for the end to come according to Christ's prophecy in Matthew 24:14. That means all the believers in Christ in the world must focus on finishing the Great Commission in this generation by evangelizing every unreached frontier people group to see the end come and witness the second coming of Christ.

Therefore, true eagle Christians must read the Bible every day and meditate on the word of God day and night. Then, we will not fall into the temptations of the devil and many false doctrines of counterfeit ministers in the world.

ARISE IN THE POWER OF THE HOLY SPIRIT

The Holy Spirit has been calling God's sons and daughters to arise and shine the light and glory of the Lord to this ever-darkening world and people under the bondages of the devil. The children of God must not focus on darkness and what the people in darkness do or do not do. They must not fill their minds with negative, condemning, criticizing, or judgmental thoughts that will open doors for the spirit of fear to enter and torment them with the power of darkness. Instead, they must arise in the name of Jesus Christ and begin to shine His light to the dark world by not only preaching the gospel but also demonstrating God's power in action to set people under the bondage of darkness free. Let's examine the following meanings of the word *arise* according to Merriam Webster's dictionary:

- **Come into existence; take on form or shape**: The children of the living God must come into existence to fulfill the main purpose of why they have been born-again in Christ for such a time as this. They have to take on the form or shape of Christ to fulfill His creation mandate for their lives each day for His glory. They were created to carry God's image and likeness according to Genesis 1:26.

    Also, 1 Corinthians 6:19-20 states *"Or do you not know that **your body is the temple of the Holy Spirit** who is in you, whom you have from God, and you are not your own? For you were bought at a price; therefore **glorify God in your body and in your spirit, which are God's**"* If a believer's body is a temple of the Holy Spirit, then he must take on the form or shape of Christ to exercise His authority and to demonstrate the power of the Holy Spirit to preach, teach, heal the sick, cast out demons, and even raise the dead for the people who dwell in the darkness.

- **Come to attention or become relevant:** Unfortunately, the post-Christian Western world lost their first love for Christ and became irrelevant to be His witness to the new generation of young people. The Church lost God's power and began to produce powerless disciples (or rather church members), who cannot transform the dying, suffering, lost, struggling, and unbelieving souls with the powerful messages of the cross and the power of the Holy Spirit.

    Therefore, children of God must arise and shine the light of Christ to the dark world with very relevant messages of the power of the Holy Spirit just like the stories in the book of Acts. The postmodern cultures and people are not interested in dead religious messages and program-based activities of the Church, but are looking for the genuine movement of God with signs, wonders, and miracles following.

- **Get on one's feet from a sitting or sleeping position:** The *Kairos* [the right, critical, opportune, God appointed moment] time has come for the believers in Christ to get out of their sleeping or sitting positions and arise and begin to shine the light of God into the dark world. Christians need to shake off spiritually self-centered, lukewarm, irrelevant, and ear-tickling messages and be filled with the Holy Spirit to become the witnesses of Christ from our own Jerusalem to the ends of the earth until Jesus Christ comes back. They must be on fire for Jesus Christ to bring His revival to the dark post-Christian world. They must not keep complaining about the dark world, the government, and what the lukewarm churches are doing or not doing because the darkness will never repent and become the light. If Christians will shine the true light of Christ into the dark world, the light of God will swallow up the darkness and transform people under the influence of darkness.

- **Renounce a former allegiance:** In order for Christians to truly arise and shine the light of God, they have to renounce any former allegiance to lukewarm, sinful, powerless, and carnal lifestyles and postmodern belief systems. In the book of Revelation, Jesus Christ warns the churches to renounce the former allegiances to the worldly belief systems and praises the faithful church. He describes the churches as the loveless church, the persecuted church, the compromising church, the corrupt church, the dead church, the faithful church, and the lukewarm church.

    Unfortunately, many postmodern Christian churches demonstrate their clear allegiance with the secular humanistic belief system to embrace all sorts of sinful practices and lifestyles as their newly adopted core tenets of faith by becoming compromising, lukewarm, and dead churches and denominations. Therefore, Jesus Christ warns in Revelation 2:5, *"Remember therefore from where you have fallen; repent and do the first works, or else I will come to you quickly and remove your lampstand from its place—unless you repent."*

It is God's appointed time for the followers of Jesus Christ to arise from the former ways of complacency, lukewarmness, religiosity, compromising status, faithlessness, and powerlessness to truly shine the light of Christ into the dark world for His glory. Jesus Christ commands His followers to shine the light of God to others in Matthew 5:14-16:

> *"You are the light of the world. A city that is set on a hill cannot be hidden. Nor do they light a lamp and put it under a basket, but on a lampstand, and it gives light to all who are in the house.* **Let your light so shine before men, that they may see your good works and glorify your Father in heaven.**"

During the COVID worldwide pandemic season, we constantly heard much negative news generated by news medias and government authorities. Of course, we must be wise and take all the necessary precautions so that we will not be infected with the COVID-19 virus and not infect others. However, we, the believers in Christ, must not be bound by spirits of fear generated by COVID or any other pandemic to be immobilized, but we need to arise and shine the light and glory of God to our loved ones, friends, and those who are lost in this dark world.

During that season, the Holy Spirit instructed me not to listen to worldly news media anymore, so I got rid of my Facebook, Instagram, Twitter, and LinkedIn accounts. Then, I realized how many hours that I used to spend watching and checking the above mediums to satisfy my desires to know more about worldly news and posts of friends in those platforms. If the Lord allows me to reactive them, then I will only use those platforms to glorify His name. After getting rid of them, I found the true source of peace through relying on the word of God in the Bible, praying in the Spirit to know the mind of Christ and will of God for my life each day.

I began to hear, much more clearly, the still small voice of the Holy Spirit. I was able to find the true wisdom and guidance through having communion with the Prince of Peace, Yeshua (the true name of Jesus in Hebrew) who lives in me.

We can read and claim Psalm 91 every day, but we may not see the manifestation of the fruit of God's promises in our lives if our hearts are filled with fear, doubt, worry, anxiety, unbelief, and faithlessness. However, if we totally rely on the divine peace that has been generated by the Prince of Peace who lives inside of us, then we can truly experience the fruits of His peace guiding us each step of our journey of life. Only then, can we rejoice in the Lord according to His promises in Philippians 4:4-7:

> *"Rejoice in the Lord always. Again I will say, rejoice! Let your gentleness be known to all men. The Lord is at hand.* **Be anxious for nothing***, but in everything by prayer and supplication, with thanksgiving, let your requests be made known to God; and* ***the peace of God, which surpasses all understanding, will guard your hearts and minds through Christ Jesus.****"*

- **Rejoice in the Lord always:** When the devil comes into your life to steal, to kill, and to destroy everything God has appointed for you to live the creation mandate, it is very difficult to rejoice if your eyes are focused on the darkness that the devil has been bringing to your life. In order for us to truly rejoice in the Lord always, we must choose to fix our eyes on Yeshua and appropriate His divine peace over every troubled water in our souls. If the Prince of Peace controls your heart and mind, then you will find His divine peace over all circumstances, and you can rejoice in the Lord always for His glory. Even though persecution and opposition may come from the devil, we can rejoice continually because the Lord is with us. Because our reward in Christ is great, reserved for us unto the Day when He who is our Life shall appear, and we shall be with Him in glory forever.[20]

- **Be anxious for nothing:** One of the definitions of anxiety is characterized by extreme uneasiness of the mind or brooding fear about some contingency (by Merriam-Webster). We can become very anxious about everything if we focus on the reports of any deadly sicknesses, crimes, and deaths by news media.

    If the statistics of the deaths caused by these diseases are the main reason for the lock-down of the whole country or cities, then the government authorities and media should spend equal or even greater time to warn the citizens about other causes of deaths by diseases—such as heart disease and cancer. According to the report by the *WebMD Cancer Center* (www.webmd.com/cancer), about 600,000 cancer deaths happen in the U. S. each year.[21]

    According to the report of the *World Health Organization*, cardio-vascular diseases are the leading cause of death globally, taking an estimated 17.9 million lives each year. According to the report of New York State Department of Health, about 697,000 people in the U. S. die from heart disease every year. Also, Centers for Disease Control and Prevention stated that flu resulted in 9 million to 41 million illnesses, 140,000 to 710,000 hospitalizations and 12,000 to 52,000 deaths annually between 2010 and 2020.[22] According to Worldometer's report, since the beginning of the COVID pandemic, there have been 111,820,082 total cases in the U. S. and 1,219,487 deaths (it is 1 percent of the total COVID infected people) by April, 2024.[23]

However, the word of God commends us to be anxious for nothing. In order for us to do that, our eyes must be fixed on God and His promises in the word of God. The worst thing that can ever happen to us (believers in Christ) is heaven. Because we are in Jesus Christ, we never die but enter into His glory land when our physical bodies die. Therefore, we must not be anxious for anything but trust in the Lord in all circumstances.

- **Let the peace of God guard our hearts and minds in Christ Jesus:** If we understand the power of the promise of Christ in John 14:20, we can embrace the peace of God that proceeds out of the Prince of Peace. Jesus Christ declares in John 14:20, *"At that day you will know that **I am in My Father, and you in Me, and I in you**.*" The Scripture promises that a believer will be inside of Christ, and He will be inside of the believer once one is born-again in Him. If we, the believers in Christ, are inside of the Prince of Peace, then there will not be any room for anxieties or fears to coexist. Inside of Christ is a Satan and demon free zone, power of sin free zone, sickness free zone, curse free zone, fear of death free zone. If Jesus Christ is inside of us, then He brings the authority, power, and freedom of the Kingdom of Heaven inside of us so we can live a victorious life in Him. Then, the peace of God that is flowing out of the Prince of Peace will guard our hearts and minds in Christ and we can overcome any attacks of the devil all the days of our earthly lives. If God is for us, then who can truly be against us?

SHINE THE LIGHT OF CHRIST

Once we have arisen in the power of the Holy Spirit, then we need to shine His light to the dark world. The lost people in the world are existing each day to fulfill their own evil desires: the lust of the flesh, the lust of the eyes, and the pride of life. They are the gods of their own lives, choosing good and evil for themselves, totally influenced by secular humanistic ideologies. They are bound by the power of sin, physical and spiritual sicknesses, generational and other curses from this sin infested world—fear of death, illicit drugs, alcoholism, sexual addictions, demonic oppressions, depressions and others.

Some may have enough wealth to live a luxurious lifestyle of indulgence, others may survive on meager monthly salaries, and the rest of them may exist in a poverty-stricken life without joy. The devil torments them all with deceptions, manipulations, and lies to bind them with his wicked chains of worries, fear, unbelief, confusion, condemnation, judgment, divorce, curses, sicknesses, depression, suicidal thoughts, self-mutilation, etc. They constantly live under the curses of John 10:10a, *"The thief does not come except to steal, and to kill, and to destroy..."* I believe that all human beings who were born into this world have been created by the hand of God to fulfill His divine and perfect plans on the earth. However, the devil comes to steal, to kill, and to destroy God's wonderful and divine creation mandate for their lives so that they will not be used by God to bring His salvation, healing, deliverance, and life to suffering and dying souls in the world. Therefore, the ultimate goal of the devil is to someday take as many souls as he can to the eternal Lake of Fire according to God's words in Revelation 20:12-15:

> ***And I saw the dead, small and great, standing before God, and books were opened. And another book was opened, which is the Book of Life.*** *And the dead were judged according to their works, by the things which were written in the books. The sea gave up the dead who were in it, and Death and Hades delivered up the dead who were in them. And* ***they were judged, each one according to his works.*** *Then Death and Hades were cast into the lake of fire. This is the second death.* ***And anyone not found written in the Book of Life was cast into the lake of fire.***

Then, what are God's divine missions for His children to fulfill while they live their one short lives on the earth? Let's examine the purpose of the light of Christ in this dark world:

- Matthew 28:18, ***"All authority has been given to Me in heaven and on earth."*** When Jesus Christ was resurrected, He took away the authority on the earth that Satan usurped from the first Adam. Now with His authority, we can do the same works that Jesus did while He was walking on earth because He lives inside of us. With the same authority, Jesus Christ commanded us in Matthew 28:19-20, ***"Go therefore and make disciples of all the nations,*** *baptizing them in the name of the Father and of the Son and of the Holy*

Spirit, teaching them to observe all things that I have commanded you; and lo, **I am with you always**, *even to the end of the age."* Therefore, the number one priority of Christ for His followers is to go into all the world and share the message of the Kingdom of Heaven with every people group in the world.

- Luke 19:10, **"*For the Son of Man has come to seek and to save that which was lost.*"** Once again, Jesus Christ commanded in Acts 1:8, "*But **you shall receive power when the Holy Spirit has come upon you**; and you shall be witnesses to Me in Jerusalem, and in all Judea and Samaria, and to the end of the earth."* Now the followers of Jesus not only have the authority of Christ to do the works of the Kingdom of Heaven but also have the power of the Holy Spirit to expand His kingdom from our own Jerusalem to the end of the earth.

   The Son of Man, Yeshua, lives inside of us to go and do the work of seeking and saving the lost souls in this dark world. There are still 4,422 Frontier Unreached People Groups that have almost no chance of hearing about Jesus Christ from someone in their own people group.[24] Therefore, we must go out under the authority of the Lord Jesus Christ with the assurance that He is with us always, wherever we go. He dwells in us and sends us out in the power of the Holy Spirit to evangelize every Unreached People Group in the world to fulfill His prophecy in Matthew 24:14 in this generation.[25]

- Matthew 10:7-8, "*And as you go, preach, saying, '**The kingdom of heaven is at hand. Heal the sick, cleanse*** *the lepers, raise the dead, cast out demons. Freely you have received, freely give.'"* Therefore, as we go with Christ and the Holy Spirit to do the works of the Kingdom of Heaven, His signs, wonders, and miracles will follow us to set people who have been bound by the power of darkness free.

Also, Mark 16:17 states, *"And these signs will follow those who believe:* ***In My name they will cast out demons; they will speak with new tongues…they will lay hands on the sick, and they will recover.****"* We are not called to follow the signs, wonders, and miracles but to go and preach the Kingdom of Heaven to the lost souls. Then these signs will follow us. We are created to walk and live in the supernatural and to experience miracle healing, deliverance, provision, favor, and protection in Christ as a normal Christian life style.[26]

- 1 John 3:8b, ***"For this purpose the Son of God was manifested, that He might destroy the works of the devil."*** In order for Yeshua to destroy the works of the devil, He needs the followers of Christ to obey and do the works of the Kingdom of Heaven on earth wherever they may go. What are the works of the devil described in the Bible?

  They are described in 1 Corinthians 6:9-10, *"Do you not know that the unrighteous will not inherit the kingdom of God? Do not be deceived. Neither fornicators, nor idolaters, nor adulterers, nor homosexuals, nor sodomites, nor thieves, nor covetous, nor drunkards, nor revilers, nor extortioners will inherit the kingdom of God."* Yeshua wants to deliver anyone bound by any one of the above-mentioned sins. Once they are saved and delivered from their sins and bondages, then Yeshua wants them to be discipled so that they can also destroy the works of the devil in others suffering under the same bondages.

- 1 Corinthians 4:20, "*For the kingdom of God is not in word but in power.*" The Apostle Paul reinforces the scripture by stating in 1 Corinthians 2:4, "*And my speech and my preaching were **not with persuasive words of human wisdom, but in demonstration of the Spirit and of power**.*" During Christ's ministry on earth, Jesus had informed the disciples that without Him they could do nothing (John 15:5).

  Just before His ascension, when He gave them the Great Commission to convert the world, He also commanded His disciples to receive the power from on high in Luke 24:49, "*Behold, I send the Promise of My Father upon you; but tarry in the city of Jerusalem until you are **endued with power from on high**.*" He also promised, "*You shall be baptized with the Holy Spirit not many days from now*" (Acts 1:5). This baptism of the Holy Spirit, the outpouring of power from on high, is essential. Christ has expressly informed us that it is the indispensable condition of doing the work of the Kingdom of God in His name.[27]

- Matthew 23:14, "*And this gospel of the kingdom will be preached in all the world as a witness to all the nations [**ethnos**: **Gentiles, people group, families**], and then the end will come.*" That means, when every UPG has heard the gospel of the kingdom, then the end will come, and Jesus Christ will return. Therefore, all the Christian churches in the world should focus on evangelizing the rest of the UPGs by sending their missions mobilizers to equip indigenous missions' forces to be engaged in preaching the gospel to the Frontier UPGs until Jesus Christ returns.

The conclusion of what the Lord is asking us through the above commandments and scriptures is that the followers of Christ must utilize the authority of Christ and the power of the Holy Spirit to evangelize every UPG in the world. As we go and preach the message of the Kingdom of Heaven, we must destroy the works of the devil by demonstrating the power of the Holy Spirit with signs, wonders, and miracles following. Our ultimate mission is to fulfill the Great Commission become the Great Completion in our generation by evangelizing all 4,422 Frontier UPGs (according to Joshuaproject.net) in the world until Jesus Christ comes back.

In March 2018, I had a privilege to go to Siliguri, India, a city close to Bhutan. I had a team of Global Harvest Network (GHN) trainers with me, and we conducted a weeklong GHN Conference for over 70 Christian leaders from eight different unreached regions of India. During the conference, the participants were equipped and empowered to evangelize their own UPGs with signs, wonders, and miracles following. During one of the altar calls, the glory of the Lord filled the conference room and almost all the participants fell to the ground by the power of the Holy Spirit.

When they got up, they were healed of various sicknesses and received the baptism of the Holy Spirit. One brother said to me, *"Now I know how it is like to be filled with the Holy Spirit. From now on, I will go wherever the Holy Spirit leads me to go and evangelize as many UPGs as I can with the authority of Jesus Christ and the power of the Holy Spirit with signs, wonders, and miracles following."* During this trip, we also had a chance to enter Bhutan to pray for the country for a few hours. There are approximately 18,800 Christians in Bhutan (2 percent of the total population) who have been persecuted by the society and government. All Bhutanese citizens are expected to be Buddhists. Anyone who converts to Christianity faces intense pressure to return to their former religion.

Conversion is considered to bring shame on the family, and new believers are often disowned by their family members.[28] I have been doing my very best to shine the light of Christ in the world as His eagle Christian. There is not much time left before the worldwide tribulation begins according to the prophecies of the book of Revelation. The world has dramatically become darker after the release of the COVID pandemic influenced by the power of darkness.

We do not know how long we will have religious freedom even in the U.S. and the Western countries. The systematic persecution against Judeo-Christian values and the Church has intensified during the COVID season worldwide. Perhaps God has brought us into this world for such a time as this so that we can arise and shine the light of Christ from our own Jerusalem to the end of the earth. We need to become eagle Christians who will fly according to the perfect will of God to bring His salvation, healing, and deliverance to the lost souls in the world—especially to those Unreached People Groups for His glory.

Chapter 5

BE A MIRACLE MAKER

Jesus Christ is the Miracle Maker. Jesus changed water into wine in John 2:1-11. Jesus cured the son of a certain royal official who was close to death in John 4:46-47. Jesus casted out an unclean spirit in the synagogue in Capernaum in Mark 1:23-24, *"Now there was a man in their synagogue with an unclean spirit. And he cried out, saying, 'Let us alone! What have we to do with You, Jesus of Nazareth? Did You come to destroy us? I know who You are—the Holy One of God!'"*

The unclean spirit recognized Jesus Christ as the Holy One of God—the Miracle Maker for His glory. Jesus Christ also cast a legion of demons out of a man who met Him out of the tombs in Mark 5:1-20. Jesus Christ, the Miracle Maker, sent the unclean spirits to enter the herd of swine and they ran violently down the steep place into the sea, and drowned. Jesus Christ raised a dead daughter of one of the rulers of the synagogue, Jairus by name, in Mark 5:22-24, 35-42.

A certain woman who had an excessive flow of blood for twelve years had faith and touched the hem of Jesus' clothes to receive her healing in Mark 5:25-34, *"For she said, 'If only I may touch His clothes, I shall be made well."* (vs. 28). And Jesus Christ said to her, *"Daughter, your faith has made you well. Go in peace and be healed of your affliction."* (vs. 34). Jesus Christ raised Lazarus who had been dead for four days (John 11:17-44) and He declared in John 11:25-26, *"I am the resurrection and the life. He who believes in Me, though he may die, he shall live. And whoever lives and believes in Me shall never die. Do you believe this?"* He is the Miracle Maker and can bring resurrection and life to anyone who believes in Him. Jesus Christ healed a leper in Mark 1:40-42, *"Now a leper came to Him, imploring Him, kneeling down to Him and saying to Him, 'If You are willing, You can make me clean.' Then Jesus, moved with compassion, stretched out His hand and touched him, and said to him, 'I am willing; be cleansed.'"*

Jesus Christ caused the winds and waves to obey Him in Matthew 8:23-26 by simply rebuking the winds and the sea to be calm. Jesus Christ healed two blind men in Matthew 9:27-30, *"Two blind men followed Him, crying out and saying, 'Son of David, have mercy on us!' And Jesus said to them, 'Do you believe that I am able to do this?' They said to Him, 'Yes, Lord.' Then He touched their eyes, saying, 'According to your faith let it be to you.' And their eyes were opened."*

Jesus healed a deaf and mute man in Mark 7:31-37. Jesus cured a woman who had been bent over for 18 years by a spirit of infirmity in Luke 13:10-13. Jesus fed over five thousand people in Matthew 14:15-21. And Jesus Christ performed numerous other miracles, and the Apostle John stated in John 21:25, *"And there are also many other things that Jesus did, which if they were written one by one, I suppose that even the world itself could not contain the books that would be written."*

QUALIFICATIONS TO BE A MIRACLE MAKER

For us to understand how we can be Christ's miracle makers, we must fully appropriate what He accomplished for us on the cross and through His resurrection by faith:

- **Jesus conquered the power of sin** that infests all humanity by the fall of the first Adam at the cross as the Lamb of God who takes away the sin of the world (John 1;29). He became the Last Adam to break the power and bondage of sin over the first Adam's descendants by giving them a second chance to be free when they surrender their lives to Christ as their Lord and Savior (John 3:16). Therefore, you surrender your life to Christ by confessing all your sins and asking Him to wash them with His blood.

  Then He forgives all your sins and cleanses all the unrighteous deeds in your life (1 John 1:9). Once you accepted Jesus Christ as your Lord and Savior and were baptized into Christ Jesus, you were buried with Him through baptism into death (Romans 6:3-4). Therefore, our old man who was bound by the power of sin was crucified with Jesus Christ so that the body of sin might be done away with, and that we should no longer be slaves of sin (Romans 6:6).

  Since your old man was crucified with Christ, you are now born again in the power of His resurrection to live according to His perfect will, to fulfill His creation mandate for your life as a new creation in Him. Then, symbolically speaking, you are not bound anymore by the cursed DNA of the first Adam, but by the new blessed DNA of the Last Adam, Jesus Christ to have abundant life on earth and eternal life in heaven. Now, you can declare Romans 8:2, "*For the law of the Spirit of life in Christ Jesus* (the new DNA in Christ) *has made me free from the law of sin and death* (the old DNA in the first Adam)."

- **Jesus provides us with the provision for healing:** Sickness is one of the fruits manifested by the power of sin that entered into the world through the first Adam's fall. However, it is God's divine will for us to enjoy His abundant life of health as we obey His commandments and live according to His perfect will. Nevertheless, God's healing provision is conditional in nature—we must do our part according to Exodus 15:26, "*If you **diligently heed the voice of the Lord your God and do what is right in His sight, give ear to His commandments and keep all His statutes**, I will put none of the diseases on you which I have brought on the Egyptians. **For I am the Lord who heals you.**"*

    Therefore, in order for God's children to receive His divine healing, they must diligently heed the voice of the Lord; do what is right in His sight; and give ear to His commandments to keep all His statutes, then His healing power will flow upon them and heal them. Also, Isaiah 53:5 declares, "*But He* (Yeshua) *was wounded for our transgressions, He was bruised for our iniquities; the chastisement for our peace was upon Him, and **by His stripes we were healed.**"*

    For us to appropriate Christ's healing provision, we must surrender our lives to the Lord and accept the fact that He was wounded for our sins; bruised for our iniquities; and by His stripes we were healed as born-again believers in Him. If we put our sickness on the body of Christ at the cross, He has the power to heal us from all infirmities. Then, John 10:10b can be fulfilled in our lives, "*I have come that they may have life, and that they may have it more abundantly.*" I believe that we can fully appropriate Christ's abundant life without suffering under various sicknesses and live in His divine favor and blessings each day.

- **Jesus has redeemed us from the curse of the law:** Galatian 3:13-14 states, *"Christ has redeemed us from the curse of the law, **having become a curse for us** (for it is written, 'Cursed is everyone who hangs on a tree'), that **the blessing of Abraham might come upon the Gentiles in Christ Jesus**, that we might receive the promise of the Spirit through faith."* That means, if we have accepted Jesus Christ as our Lord and Savior, then the curse of the law that came upon all the descendants of the first Adam has been put on the body of Jesus at the cross. So, Jesus Christ became a curse for us as the Last Adam so that we can be totally free from the curses of the first Adam's blood and receive the blessing of Abraham through the blood of Christ in faith.

Therefore, if we are in Christ, we are not cursed any longer but blessed with all the heavenly blessings that were bestowed upon Abraham. We can boldly claim that any generational curses or any curses that anyone might have spoken against us have no power or effect on us forever. Just like Balaam declared in Numbers 23:20, *"Behold, I have received a command to bless; He has blessed, and I cannot reverse it."*; what God has blessed cannot be cursed. No one can reverse it. In order for you to be a miracle maker in Christ, you have to accept the fact that you are blessed and not cursed so you can be God's miracle maker to release His favor and blessings to those who need salvation, healing, and deliverance.

- **The resurrection of Jesus Christ empowers us to overcome the fear of death:** If anyone is a born-again believer in Christ, then someday soon, he/she will experience the promise in 1 Corinthians 15: 52, 54-55, *"In a moment, in the twinkling of an eye, at the last trumpet. For the trumpet will sound, and the dead will be raised incorruptible, and we shall be changed. So, when this corruptible has put on incorruption, and this mortal has put on immortality, then shall be brought to pass the saying that is written: '**Death is swallowed up in victory**.' O Death, where is your sting? O Hades, where is your victory?"*

  Therefore, through the death and resurrection of our Lord, Jesus Christ, He overcame the power of death to provide the children of God the same blessing of the resurrection life on earth and eternal life in heaven. *"For Christ also suffered once for sins, the just for the unjust, that He might bring us to God, being put to death in the flesh but made alive by the Spirit*" (1 Peter 3:18).

  When our mortal body experiences death, if we are in Christ, we will immediately enter the Kingdom of Heaven to be with the Lord Jesus Christ forever. The promise of God in Revelation 21:4 will be fulfilled for those who are in Christ: *"And God will wipe away every tear from their eyes**; there shall be no more death**, nor sorrow, nor crying. There shall be no more pain, for the former things have passed away."*

- **The resurrected Lion of Judah overcame the power of Satan**: Immediately after the fall of Adam, the Lord declared His divine deliverance plan in Genesis 3:15, *"And I will put enmity between you and the woman,* *and between your seed and **her Seed**; He shall bruise your head, and you shall bruise His heel.*" In this prophetic word of God, He was declaring that someday, the Deliverer (Messiah) would come out of the woman (the nation of Israel).

Her Seed (the Messiah, Jesus Christ) would bruise or crush the head of the devil and Satan would bruise His heel (at the cross). Jesus Christ also declared in John 16:33, *"In this world you will have tribulation; but be of good cheer, I have overcome the world."* The resurrection of Christ gave Him power to overcome the world that has been infested by the evil power of the devil. As Jesus Christ lives inside of His followers, they can also overcome the devil in this world through the authority of Christ and the power of the Holy Spirit.

Revelation 12:11 declares that they (believers in Christ) overcame him (Satan) by the blood of the Lamb and by the word of their testimony. Eventually, the Scripture in Revelation 20:10b declares the ultimatum to Satan, *"**The devil, who deceived them, was cast into the lake of fire and brimstone where the beast and the false prophet are. And they will be tormented day and night forever and ever.**"* Thus, Satan's final fate has already been determined in the word of God.

Jesus Christ destroyed the works of the devil at the cross and rose from the dead to dismantle the above five effects that caused every human being to suffer under the power of darkness—sin, sickness, the curse of the law, fear of death, and Satan. Whoever calls upon the name of the Lord shall be saved and will be empowered to become a miracle maker to set many others free from the same curses of the devil on the earth. Jesus Christ, the Miracle Maker dwells in us and His presence in our lives will qualify us to be His miracle makers to fulfill His commands in Matthew 10:7-8 as His eagle Christians.

HAVE ABSOLUTE FAITH IN THE LORD

Having absolute faith in the Lord will qualify anyone in Christ to become a miracle maker for His glory. Hebrews 11:6 declares, *"But without faith it is impossible to please Him, for he who comes to God must believe that He is, and that He is a rewarder of those who diligently seek Him."* Absolute faith in God is the foundational requirement for anyone who is in Christ to please Him in whatever we do for His glory.

Our simple faith in God will make us believe that He is the only answer and solution to any issue in life. When we need salvation, Yeshua (Jesus in Hebrew) is our salvation; when we need deliverance, He is our Deliverer; when we need healing, He is our Healer, etc. All of us need to look to God for our answers. Every problem has a solution, not in abstract logic, but in the living God and He meets all of us at the point of our need.[29]

We cannot have faith in the Lord when we do not seek Him with all our hearts and minds to know His perfect will for every question that we have in life. We must not just render our prayers to God by merely pouring out our heart to Him, but we must also intentively wait on the Lord to hear Him clearly on any issue. If we don't distinctly hear His answers to our prayers, we cannot truly move in faith to be His miracle makers to do His work because we haven't appropriated His perfect will. God rewards those who diligently seek Him every day.

Where Eagles Fly!

Romans 10:17 is the answer on how to have faith in God: *"So then faith comes by hearing, and hearing by the **word** [**rhema**: revelatory revealed] of God."* Therefore, we must read and meditate on the Word of God until His *logos* (total inspired Word of God) becomes *rhema* for our specific prayers so that we can have His assurance to act in faith. When we hear His *rhema* which gives us His gift of faith to carry out His mission on earth, then His power will manifest through us to be His miracle makers with signs, wonders, and miracles following.

Whenever we accomplish God's mission on earth, we must always humble ourselves and know that *"for it is God who works in you both to will and to do **for His good pleasure*** (Philippians 2:13)." Whatever He does through us will always be for His own good pleasure and not for our own pleasure. That means we must not judge God based on the outcome of our prayers even though it may be totally different than what we expected. God is perfect, He has no flaws, His ways are quite different than our ways, and He does not make any mistakes. I have witnessed over the years that quite a few people walked away from God when their prayers for their loved ones to be healed did not happen and they died from their illnesses.

For believers in Christ, death is not a defeat, but an ultimate victory because they are then totally free from any sufferings of this life and enter paradise in heaven according to Revelation 21:4, *"And God will wipe away every tear from their eyes; there shall be no more death, nor sorrow, nor crying. There shall be no more pain, for the former things have passed away."* Also, Psalms 116:15 declares, *"Precious in the sight of the Lord is the death of His saints."* Therefore, we must not walk away from God when He takes away our loved ones through sicknesses, but rather thank Him for delivering them from any more sufferings in this life because they are completely healed according to God's perfect will. Of course, we want to have our loved ones to stay with us longer by God healing them supernaturally, and I have witnessed Him deliver multitudes of sick people from many different deadly diseases in the world. However, God's will may be different than our will at times, and He may decide His children not to suffer any longer by taking them to His eternal home. As we have faith to be His miracle makers, we need to realize that whatever we do is to please Him and to fulfill His perfect will on earth and not ours.

FAITH THAT WORKS

Everyone has a measure of faith according to Romans 12:3b, *"as God has allotted to each **a measure of faith** (NASB)."* Therefore, as we become mature in the Lord, the measure of faith in us will also grow accordingly based on our experiences of utilizing our faith to work. There is also a gift of faith through the manifestation of the Spirit based on 1 Corinthians 12:9, *"to another **faith by the same Spirit**."*

I have experienced supernatural miracles taking place during my mission trips to the nations when the gift of faith from the Holy Spirit came down upon me to be mixed with my measure of faith. In other words, my measure of faith had to be in line with the gift of faith through the power of the Holy Spirit for His miracle to be released through me.

Therefore, our faith resting on our own measure of faith that has been generated by our own willpower (the strength of will to carry out one's decisions, wishes, or plans) and desire will not produce His miracles. Therefore, Hebrews 4:2b warns us, *"but the word which they heard did not profit them, **not being mixed with faith** in those who heard it."* Ultimately, our faith must be mixed with the authority of Christ and power of the Holy Spirit through the gift of faith from above to produce His miracles. Then, what kinds of faith do we need to possess to make it work?

- **We must have *"Now faith"* according to Hebrews 11:1**: *"Now faith is the substance of things hoped for, the evidence of things not seen."* *"The substance of things hoped for"* is a past tense: what we have been praying for in the past. *"Now faith"* is a present tense: faith that we believe at this present moment will cause us to expect our miracles to manifest in God's appointed future. *"The evidence of things not seen"* is a future tense: we believe that what we have been praying in faith now will happen as the evidence of things not seen in the near future. However, now faith that is totally guided by the Holy Spirit and the perfect will of Christ alone will work for those who are seeking first the Kingdom of God and His righteousness.

- **Be assured of the faith in God**: It is God's divine will for us to enjoy our life of faith in Him so that we can appropriate His blessings, anointing, and power to be His miracle maker. Above all we should take the shield of faith because faith preserves us from all sorts of wicked schemes of the enemies.[30] Once we put our total faith in God, then we can boldly receive His assurance and promises in Ephesians 3:20, *"Now to Him who is able to do exceedingly abundantly above all that we ask or think, **according to the power that works in us.**"*

- **Embrace the faith in Christ to become His miracle maker**: *"For it is God who works in you both to will and to do for His good pleasure."* (Philippians 2:13). Once we embrace the faith in Him, we can totally trust that He will work through us to accomplish His perfect will through our lives on earth. If we do not have faith in Him, then we will try to figure out God's mission in our lives according to our own wisdom and power. Then, the final result will be to manifest our own good pleasure using the name of Christ and Scriptures—we will eventually build our own kingdom work on earth in His name.

- **Confess the faith according to the Word of God**: No matter how difficult a task we may face, we must trust the Lord in faith and declare that we can do all things through Christ who strengthens us (Philippians 4:13). Without believing the Scriptures that can strengthen our faith in God, we will not be able to move in action to make our faith produce His miracles in our lives and for others. If we could only have faith in the Word of God, truly we can do all things through Christ to be His miracle makers to expand His kingdom on earth.

- **Show your faith by your works**: If we have faith in God to be His miracle makers, then we must do and act on it to produce His great works in action to fulfill His divine will on earth. James 2:17-18 states, *"Thus also **faith by itself, if it does not have works, is dead**. But someone will say, 'You have faith, and I have works.' Show me your faith without your works, and I will show you my faith by my works."* We must not just attend a church, but we need to be His church—His miracle making *ecclesia* (a living stone or living and moving His kingdom station on the earth).

YOUR FAITH IN GOD HAS TO BE GREATER THAN YOUR FEAR

For us to become Christ's miracle makers, we must have greater faith in Him than that of any fear of darkness. We must move by our *now faith* to achieve what we have been believing for in the near future just like Hebrews 11:1 declares, *"Now faith is the substance of things hoped for, the evidence of things not seen."* If our faith in God is greater than any fear of not experiencing the fruit of our prayers, then He will move heaven and earth to allow us to taste our prayers to be answered in His perfect way, time, and will.

However, if our faith in God and our fear of failure is of equal level, then we will experience very conditional outcomes: if we are moving in faith, then we will experience His divine victory, but if we are controlled by fear, then we will taste defeat no matter how hard we try to overcome it. The devil is an expert at sowing his fear thoughts into our heart so that we will be defeated by the fear that we have repeatedly rehearsed in our heart. As Proverbs 23:7 states, *"For as he thinks in his heart, so is he."*

Therefore, we must continuously fill our hearts with faith words of the Bible and meditate on them day and night. Faith thoughts in our hearts brings God's victory in our lives and empower us to become His miracle makers for His glory. If our faith in God is much lower than the fears the devil has instilled in our heart, then what we have feared the most will begin to manifest in our life. Job 3:25 declares, *"For the thing I greatly feared has come upon me, and what I dread has happened to me.*" For example: suppose you become sick and go to see a doctor, who is an expert in the type of disease, and he declares after he examines you thoroughly that you will only live for six months to a year. If you believe what the doctor says as the truth and put your faith in his words, then I believe that what you fear the most, according to the doctor's prediction, can happen to you in six months to a year.

However, you are a man of faith and when you put your total trust in the words of God in the Bible, and you consider what the doctor had said as **a truth** yet decide to put complete faith in the Lord and declare **the Truth**, "*by whose (Christ's) stripes, you were healed*" (1 Peter 2:24b) over your life, then you can be cured based on your total faith in the living Word of God.

To be God's miracle makers, we must raise our level of faith higher than the many fears the enemy tries to throw at us when we try to become God's miracle makers. Without faith, we cannot please God and will never be able to carry out His miracle missions in life. Having faith in God means that you will hear the still small voice of the Holy Spirit and obey His direction and commandments. There is one common denominator among the heroes in the Bible—they had very close communion with the Holy Spirit and obeyed whatever the Lord directed them to do for His good pleasure.

OBEY THE VOICE OF THE HOLY SPIRIT

It is the prerequisite to obey the voice of the Lord prior to experiencing His victory in our life in faith, according to Exodus 15:26, *"**If you diligently heed the voice of the Lord your God and do what is right in His sight**, give ear to His commandments and keep all His statutes, I will put none of the diseases on you which I have brought on the Egyptians. **For I** *am the Lord who heals you.*" As we are led by the still small voice of the Holy Spirit, He will guide us into all truth and show us how to appropriate God's divine life of victory, healing, and deliverance to be His miracle makers to set others free in the name of Jesus Christ. Also, we can taste God's divine healing according to 1 Peter 2:24 if we are willfully choosing to live by the principle of *"having died to sins, and might live for righteousness."* Then the power of His words—"*by whose stripes you were healed"* will manifest in our lives.

You may question God's healing power because you have not received His divine healing even though you have believed in the promise of 1 Peter 2:24 for many years, but you have not seen the fruit of your faith. You can become discouraged and say, *"If God heals me in His time, that will be great; however, if He chooses not to heal me, then it is alright because I will be healed when I get to heaven."*

You may also have been praying for a loved one to be healed for a long time, but she dies with a disease. Now, you may feel that God did not hear your prayers, and you may question Him why would He allow her to die or take her away from you? You can even be angry with God and walk away from Him because He did not answer your prayer as you wished Him to do for you.

As Isaiah 55:8-9 states, "***For My thoughts are not your thoughts, nor are your ways My ways, says the Lord.*** *For as the heavens are higher than the earth, so are My ways higher than your ways and My thoughts than your thoughts."* Also, Philippians 2:13 declares, *"for it is God who works in you both to will and to do **for His good pleasure**."* Therefore, ultimately God decides the outcome of our prayers according to His perfect thoughts, ways, and for His good pleasure and not for our own good pleasure. Then, how do we follow the command of Christ in Matthew 10:7-8, *"And as you go, preach, saying,*

'The kingdom of heaven is at hand. **Heal the sick, cleanse the lepers, raise the dead, cast out demons**. *Freely you have received, freely give."* Jesus Christ also declared in Mark 16:15-18, *"And He said to them, 'Go into all the world and preach the gospel to every creature. He who believes and is baptized will be saved; but he who does not believe will be condemned.* ***And these signs will follow those who believe: In My name they will cast out demons; they will speak with new tongues****; they will take up serpents; and if they drink anything deadly, it will by no means hurt them;* ***they will lay hands on the sick, and they will recover."***

We can confirm that it is God's will for His children to be engaged in destroying the works of the devil (1 John 3:8b). Wherever God asks His children to go, they need to preach the Kingdom of God, heal the sick, and cast out demons in the name of Jesus Christ. We must obey His commandments and pray according to His perfect will for those who are lost, sick, and in bondage under demonic powers. When we pray for someone to be healed, then we need to have faith in God to move in His miracle power to heal the sick. How long should we pray for a sick person? The answer is that we need to pray for the sick person until His miracle healing manifests in him or her.

How about if the person is not healed but dies with the sickness? If the sick person was a born-again believer in Christ, then God answered the saint's prayers for him/her to be totally healed in heaven where there is no more sickness or death. Once again, for any believer in Christ, death is not a defeat but the ultimate victory in Christ. If you have been praying for believers in Christ to be healed, but they die, then that is the ultimate healing and victory for them in Christ. We need to pray for their living family members to be comforted by the Holy Spirit. But, at the same time, we can rejoice in the

Lord that their suffering on earth is over and they have entered into the glory land for eternity. Then you can move on to pray for others to be healed. When I was serving the Lord at a church as one of the Elders, a retired pastor was suffering with the last stage of cancer. Many other leaders and members of the church prophesied that he would be healed and live to be over 90 years old (he was 84 years old at the time). When I came back home from my mission trip, the leaders of the church asked me to visit him and pray for his healing. So, I went to his home and was about to pray for his divine healing.

Suddenly the Holy Spirit whispered in my ear that He would take him to heaven within two weeks. After I heard that from Him, I wasn't able to pray for his healing, but I prayed in my heart that God would take his pain away from his body until the appointed day of his departure to heaven. As the Holy Spirit had spoken to me, he went to be with the Lord within two weeks. We can only exercise our faith in line with the perfect will of God for anyone to be healed. But we must not allow our faith to be diminished because the Lord doesn't answer our prayers for healing quickly. The truth in 1 Peter 2:24 must not be nullified by a truth of how you are currently still sick and not healed yet.

ENCOUNTERS WITH THE MIRACLE MAKER

By the grace of God, I have had the privilege of traveling to more than 100 countries to represent the Light of God, Jesus Christ, in the dark world for the past 37 years. Over the years of doing His mission works in the nations, I have learned one of the most important lessons surrendering my spirit, soul, flesh, heart, and mind to the Lord Jesus Christ so that He can do all things through me for His glory. We must remember that it is God who works in us for His good pleasure according to Philippians 2:13. Therefore, whatever we do for God, the focus of our work is to do His will and to do it all for His good pleasure. All we need to do is to be available for the Miracle Maker, who resides inside of us, to manifest Himself through us to save, heal, and deliver the lost, hurting, suffering, and dying souls in the world. As we allow Him to do that through us, we are a candidate to become His miracle maker for His glory. Now, I would like to share with you some of the miracles that I personally experienced in the nations when the Miracle Maker manifested Himself through me in the mission fields in the past:

With Underground Church Leaders: I was ministering to over 250 underground church leaders from a closed Asian country at a secret location in the spring of 2012. I was teaching them from 8:30 a.m. till 5:00 p.m. each day for 10 days. It was a small space where over 250 young people were packed in without any space between them. One afternoon session, I asked them if there were anyone who needed God's supernatural healing. 67 people raised their hands and explained to me what kinds of miracle healing they needed.

I did not have any space to move closer to personally pray for them. So, I asked them to stand up and put their hands over where they were hurting in their bodies to receive their healing in faith and I began praying for them. After I was petitioning the Lord to heal them for about five minutes, I opened my eyes to look around. Suddenly, the meeting room was filled with a strange fog so I could not see them clearly. I thought my glasses had become foggy, so I took them off to clean them, but I realized that it was not my glasses. I began to feel the very strong presence of God in the room, so I turned around and asked my interpreter if she was feeling what I was experiencing at that moment. She said to me, *"Yes! I feel the glory of God in the room."* Then, she just collapsed to the ground. At the same moment, all 67 of them began to fall to the ground by the power of God. I was hardly able to stand and could not talk for another 45 minutes.

After 45 minutes passed, they began to get up one by one and testified that all of them were supernaturally healed by the Miracle Maker who showed up with His glory in the room. Truly, Jesus Christ reveals the glory of God through us to destroy the works of the devil according to 2 Corinthians 4:6, *"For it is the God who commanded light to shine out of darkness, who has shone in our hearts to give the light of the knowledge of the glory of God in the face of Jesus Christ."* and 1 John 3:8b, *"For this purpose the Son of God was manifested, that He might destroy the works of the devil."*

Blind eyes opened in Pleven, Bulgaria: I conducted an open-air meeting at Pleven City Center Park in July 1992. Over 250 local people showed up for the event. During the altar call, over 100 people surrendered their hearts to the Lord. When I asked them if there was anyone who needed God's supernatural healing, a middle-aged lady came to me escorted by her two friends and asked me to pray for her so her blind eyes would be opened. At first, I was nervous because it was the very first time anyone with blind eyes asked me to pray for healing.

As I was praying for her eyes to be opened, the Holy Spirit whispered in my ears and said to me, *"Put your hands on her eyes and rebuke the spirit of infirmity in the name of Jesus Christ!"* So, I did just that and suddenly she began to jump and scream with all her might. I asked my interpreter what she was screaming about, and she told me that she was saying, *"I *can see!*" I was overjoyed with the miracle of her supernatural healing. After that another 100 plus people came to me for their healing, so I stayed at the park to pray for everyone who was sick in the name of Jesus Christ until 11:30 p.m. The Miracle Maker showed up and healed many people that night. I realized that night that I was nothing but Christ's microphone. As He picked me up and spoke through me, He had power to save, heal, and deliver any souls who He had been appointed to be touched by His miracle working power.

A lady healed of her broken back: I was conducting revival meetings at a church in Atlanta, GA in May 2007. During the altar call, Mrs. Jung came to be prayed for in her wheelchair because her back was broken in three places due to a recent car accident in February. She was in great pain and was desperate to receive God's miracle healing. I sincerely prayed for her divine healing with all my heart.

I anointed her with oil and commanded her broken back be healed in the name of Jesus Christ. She suddenly got up from her wheelchair and fell forward to the ground. She was in the floor for about 20 minutes under the power of the Holy Spirit. When she got up, she was totally healed and without any pain. She danced before the Lord with tears of joy flowing down her face. The Miracle Maker touched her through me and she was restored.

A young lady's scoliosis healed in Ukraine: I ministered at Youth in Action camp in Ternopil, Ukraine in July 2016. A 16-year-old young lady came to me and my wife, Margarita, to pray for her back with a scoliosis problem. As we were praying for her, we noticed that her left leg was ½ inch shorter than her right leg, so we asked the Lord to heal her completely by rebuking the spirit of infirmity and commanding it to depart from her. Suddenly, the power of God came upon her, and she fell to the floor and when she got up, she was totally healed, and her left leg grew out to match with her right leg.

Jonathan miraculously healed in Colombia: Margarita and I were ministering at Community of Faith Church in Turbaco, Colombia in May 2018. After the revival meeting was over, we were resting at a guest home. One young man brought his friend, Jonathan, who had been badly injured by being pinned between a bus and a truck for two hours. Through the accident, three of his ribs, his pelvic bone, and five vertebrae were broken. Also, the tendons of his right foot were badly torn. When he came to us, he was in great pain. As we began to pray for him, demons in him started to manifest so we had to cast out the demons first.

After we cast out many demons in Jonathan, he was able to accept the Lord Jesus Christ as his Savior. Then, we prayed for his healing and the power and presence of God came upon him and he was totally healed. He came to the service that we were ministering at another Community of Faith Church in Cartagena and testified of his divine healing. Through his miracle healing, all seven of his family members who came to the service were saved and many others were healed after hearing about his divine miracle healing.

A young lady's deaf ears opened in Bishkek, Kyrgyzstan: I conducted Global Harvest Network (GHN) seminars to equip and empower Russian, Kyrgyz, Uzbek, Tatar, and Kurdish Christians who came for the seminars in Bishkek. Two other pastors and I also went and ministered at a secret home gathering in the Southern region which took more than 14 hours to reach by car from the capital city. During this trip, the Holy Spirit supernaturally moved and healed over 30 people who had been suffering with back pains, knee problems, impaired hearing, crippled legs, etc. One young lady whose ears were both 80% deaf was miraculously healed at one meeting. Surely, Jesus Christ is the Miracle Maker who lives inside of us in order to empower us to become His miracle makers as we are engaging in His kingdom work in the U.S. and around the world.

Jesus declares in 1 John 3:8b, "*For this purpose the Son of God was manifested, that **He might destroy the works of the devil**.*" What are the works of the devil? 1) Satan, through his deception, lies, and manipulation tactics, deceives as many souls as he can to take them to eternal hell with him. 2) He torments people by inflicting them with sicknesses, curses, addictions, bondages, demonic oppressions, spirits of fear, depression, hopelessness, unforgiveness, etc. 3) He creates false belief systems to entice people to follow his wicked schemes to rise up against God ordained principles in the Bible such as woke and liberal agendas of darkness.

Therefore, Jesus Christ wants us to be His anointed miracle makers to join with Him in destroying the works of the devil each day, just like all the followers of Christ did in the book of Acts. Jesus Christ cannot accomplish His mission of destroying the works of the devil without His disciples joining with Him in His divine kingdom work. Jesus Christ absolutely needs each of us to do His kingdom work on earth as much as we need Him to help our personal issues in life to be resolved. Let us arise and shine the light of Christ in this dark world as His eagle Christians who are ready to be engaged in His divine missions of setting the lost, wounded, suffering, dying souls in the world free for His glory.

Chapter 6

BE MORE THAN A CONQUEROR

W*ho shall separate us from the love of Christ? Shall tribulation, or distress, or persecution, or famine, or nakedness, or peril, or sword? Yet in all these things we are more than conquerors through Him who loved us* (Romans 8:35, 37). In order for us to be more than conquerors in Christ, we must first deal with our old man who has been under the curses of the first Adam. When we are constantly under the bondages of old habits, sinful natures, addictions to worldly substances and pleasures, entertaining shame and guilt of the past, and negative thought patterns, then we can never become more than conquerors in Christ. For us to call ourselves "more than conquerors," we must start overcoming our old natures through the power of the indwelling Holy Spirit in us whenever we face the temptations of the demonic forces of darkness.

How can we deal with our old man who has been bound by the body of sin ever since the fall of the first Adam? Romans 5:12 states, *"Therefore, just as through one man sin entered the world, and death through sin, and thus death spread to all men, because all sinned..."* Unfortunately, every human being that has ever been born into this world has inherited the DNA of the first Adam as his physical descendants. What kinds of behaviors come from the cursed DNA of the first Adam inflicted by the power of darkness through the fallen angel, Lucifer? The cursed natures of the fallen mankind include: unbelief, doubt, worry, fear, jealousy, judgment, self-righteousness, condemnation, critical and negative spirits, evil thoughts, the lust of the eyes, the lust of the flesh, the pride of life, sexual perversion, immorality, murderous thoughts, evil imaginations, unforgiveness, etc. Every living person, including believers in Christ, has to deal constantly with some if not all of the above thoughts each day. Prior to the fall of Adam and Eve, they enjoyed the perfect fellowship with the living God because they were governed by the righteous and holy DNA of the Creator Himself—as they were created to carry the image and likeness of Him in all manners of their lives.

However, when sin entered into Adam through the deception of Satan, his DNA was altered (symbolically speaking) and the descendants of Adam began to behave as the sons of darkness rather than light. Therefore, Romans 3:23 declares, *"for all have sinned and fall short of the glory of God."* That means, when the first Adam sinned, he lost and fell short of the glory of God.

In like manner, when we sin, we too fall short of the glory of God and will lose His favor, blessings, and presence in our lives. As the consequence, the power of darkness begins to control our minds and hearts to follow the ways of the world and ultimately of Satan. The tragic reality is that a fallen man cannot deliver himself from the body of sin by using willpower, meditation, behavior modification technics or religious rituals because the fundamental issues are based on the altered and marred DNA.

As a result, God Himself provided the solution for fallen mankind by sending His own begotten Son, Jesus Christ, as the last Adam to die on the cross to pay the penalty of sin for all humanity. Thus, Romans 6:23 declares, *"For the wages of sin is death, but the gift of God is eternal life in Christ Jesus our Lord."* That means all descendants of Adam have sinned and fallen very short of the glory of God—removed from His presence forever if they do not accept the gift of God, Jesus Christ. Romans 5:18-19 reaffirms this, *"Therefore, as through one man's (the first Adam) offense judgment came to all men, resulting in condemnation, even so **through one Man's (Jesus Christ) righteous act the free gift came to all men, resulting in justification of life.** For as by one man's disobedience many were made sinners, so also by one Man's obedience many will be made righteous."*

Jesus Christ came to deliver the fallen descendants of Adam back to the glory and presence of God. And He bore the wages of the sin of all humanity and paid the death penalty for all at the cross. He was the sinless Son of the living God, and the grave and all the power of darkness could not hold Him dead underground. Jesus Christ was resurrected after paying for the mankind's penalty of death to provide the gift of God— eternal life in Christ Jesus our Lord. Jesus Christ became the new and last Adam who provides new DNA for every fallen man who will surrender his life to Him as his Lord and Savior.

The bottom line is very clear in that if you live under the cursed DNA and blood type of the first Adam, you will surely die in your sins and fall into hell and pay for those sins eternally. However, if you receive Jesus Christ as your Lord and Savior, then His blood will flow in your body with the new blessed DNA of the last Adam activated in your life. Life is in the blood and in order for the fallen descendants of the first Adam to have eternal life, symbolically speaking, we need the transfusion of the holy and pure blood of Christ in our lives. Then new DNA of the last Adam will be activated to provide eternal life in heaven and abundant life on the earth as God's eagle Christians to shine His light and glory to the lost souls in this dark world.

THE OLD MAN FACTOR

The old man in every descendant of the first Adam is the one who commits sins guided by the cursed blood and DNA of the fallen one. In order for Christ to deliver the fallen sinners, He not only had to die on the cross for the sins of the world as the Lamb of God but also crucified the old man in all of us with Him so that the body of sin might be done away with according to Romans 6:3-6, "*Or do you not know that as many of us as were baptized into Christ Jesus were baptized into His death? Therefore,* **we were buried with Him through baptism into death,** *that just as Christ was raised from the dead by the glory of the Father, even so* **we also should walk in newness of life***. For if we have been united together in the likeness of His death certainly, we also shall be in the likeness of His resurrection, knowing this, that* **our old man was crucified with Him, that the body of sin might be done away with,** *that we should no longer be slaves of sin.*"

That means we cannot tame, educate, alter, or deliver the nature of DNA of our old man who had been cursed under the initial sin of the first Adam. God had to send the New and Last Adam, Jesus Christ, to die on the cross not only to take away our sins but also to crucify the sinner—the old man with Him at the cross so that the body of sin might be destroyed.

Thus, when we were water baptized, our old man was dead with Christ as we go under the water and we were born again in Christ as we came out of the water. So, the promise of 2 Corinthians 5:17 has been fulfilled: "*Therefore, if anyone is in Christ,* **he is a new creation***; old things have passed away; behold,* **all things have become new.**" Once we are born-again in Christ, the new DNA of Christ has activated in us through the fruit of the Holy Spirit in Galatians 5:22-23, "*But the fruit of the Spirit is love, joy, peace, longsuffering, kindness, good-*

ness, faithfulness, gentleness, self-control. Against such there is no law." Through the indwelling power of the Holy Spirit, we can overcome every temptation of the devil in our lives because our bodies have become temples of the Holy Spirit.

Therefore, if we try to crucify our old man on the cross with our own willpower, it may only last a few weeks to months until we fall again into the habits of sinful natures. **We must accept the truth in Romans 6:3-9 and declare that our old man was already crucified with Christ, then your new freedom in Christ with His new DNA will be activated.** In so doing that, you will experience the victory of Christ in your life and become more than conquerors in Him for His glory.

ENTER INTO THE KINGDOM OF GOD ON EARTH

Once we are born again in the Spirit, we can enter the Kingdom of God according to John 3:5, *"Jesus answered, 'Most assuredly, I say to you, unless one is born of water and the Spirit, he cannot enter the kingdom of God."* But does the concept of entering the Kingdom of God only apply when a believer dies on the earth and goes to heaven? Or does the believer enter the Kingdom of God while living on earth? Jesus Christ declared in Matthew 4:17, *"Repent, for the kingdom of heaven is at hand."*

Jesus Christ started His first message on earth as declaring that His presence was the manifestation of the Kingdom of Heaven on earth. We can identify the same concept of preaching the gospel of the kingdom in Matthew 9:35, *"Then Jesus went about all the cities and villages, teaching in their synagogues, preaching* **the gospel of the kingdom,** *and* *healing every sickness and every disease among the people."* Jesus Christ brought the power of the Kingdom of Heaven down to the earth to demonstrate His kingdom power to heal every sickness and disease among the people. Jesus Christ also wants the Kingdom of Heaven to come down on earth now to do His will as it is in heaven according to His model prayer that Jesus taught His disciples in Matthew 6:10, *"**Your kingdom come. Your will be done on earth** as it is in heaven."*

Whenever we pray in the name of Jesus Christ, we must expect His kingdom power to come down upon any earthly matters and to resolve them according to the perfect will of God in heaven. Our prayer must draw all the power of the Kingdom of Heaven to set anyone who is suffering on the earth free in the name of Jesus Christ. Otherwise, Jesus Christ would not have commanded His disciples to carry out His mission on earth in Matthew 10:7-8, *"And as you go, preach, saying, '**The kingdom of heaven** is at hand.' Heal the sick, cleanse the lepers, raise the dead, cast out demons. Freely you have received, freely give."*

The above Scriptures show that the believers in Christ carry the Kingdom of God on earth to do the will of God in heaven as His representatives. After the resurrection of Jesus Christ, the Son of God delegated His mission to His disciples by giving them the same supernatural power He had exhibited on earth. **But it did not end there**. The mission and power He delegated extends to the believers of this generation so that we, too, can perform miracles, signs, and wonders in His name.[31]

How then can we be the powerful regents of God on earth and be more than conquerors in Christ? We must understand the authority of Jesus Christ and the power of the Holy Spirit. After the resurrection of Christ, He declared in Matthew 28:18, *"**All authority has been given to Me in heaven and on***

earth.*"* The Last Adam, Jesus Christ took away all the authority that Satan usurped from the first Adam and became King of Kings and Lord of Lords in heaven and on earth. Consequently, if anyone accepts Jesus Christ as their Lord and Savior, then Jesus Christ will come into them and live inside of them with the full authority in heaven and on earth. That means the authority of the Kingdom of Heaven resides inside the believer to do the perfect will of God in heaven on the earth as a disciple of Christ. However, believers in Christ do not have all authority.

Only Jesus Christ who lives inside of them has all authority. Thus, believers cannot use the name of Christ to exercise His authority at their own will. Believers can only exercise the authority that has been given to them by Christ to do the perfect will of the Father God on earth. Even Jesus Christ declares in John 5:19b, *"the Son can do nothing of Himself, bu*t *what He sees the Father do; for whatever He does, the Son also does in like manner."* If Jesus Christ can only do the works that the Father authorizes Him to do, then how much more the disciples of Christ must also do only what they are permitted to do by Christ through prayers.

THE KINGDOM OF GOD IS IN THE HOLY SPIRIT

We can clearly see that the kingdom of God is in the Holy Spirit in Romans 14:17, "***for the kingdom of God is*** *not eating and drinking, but righteousness and peace and joy **in the Holy Spirit**."* Now we need to understand how to receive the power of the Holy Spirit so that we can manifest the kingdom power to preach, heal, and deliver the lost, suffering, and dying souls in the world. Jesus Christ declares in Luke 17:21, *"For indeed,*

the kingdom of God is within you." That means the Kingdom of God will manifest its presence and glory through any believers in Christ by the power of the Holy Spirit. As Jesus Christ ascended to heaven, He stated in Acts 1:8-9, "***But you shall receive power when the Holy Spirit has come upon you; and you shall be witnesses to Me*** *in Jerusalem, and in all Judea and Samaria, and* ***to the end of the earth***. *Now when He had spoken these things, while they watched, He was taken up, and a cloud received Him out of their sight*."

Jesus Christ sent the Holy Spirit on the Day of Pentecost so that the power of the Spirit could be upon every disciple of Christ to fulfill the Great Commission in Matthew 28:18-20 and Acts 1:8 to the end of the earth. In reality, the Kingdom of God was with Jesus Christ while He was ministering on the earth. After Jesus ascended to heaven, He sent the Holy Spirit to empower every believer to be a carrier of the authority of Christ to continuously expand the Kingdom of Heaven on earth until every people group hears the Gospel, so that His prophesy in Matthew 24:14 should be fulfilled in the near future:

> "*And* ***this gospel of the kingdom*** *will be preached in all the world as a witness to* ***all the nations*** *[ethnos: people groups], and then the end will come.*"

On account of this, we must be baptized in the Holy Spirit (the Holy Spirit coming upon us) in order for us to receive His power to do the work of the Kingdom of God on earth as it is in heaven. When you accept Jesus Christ as your Lord and Savior, the Holy Spirit comes into you to seal you as the guarantee of your inheritance in Christ according to Ephesians 1:13-14:

*"In Him you also trusted, after you heard the word of truth, the gospel of your salvation; in whom also, **having believed, you were sealed with the Holy Spirit of promise**, who is the guarantee of our inheritance until the redemption of the purchased possession, to the praise of His glory."*

However, you will move in God's kingdom power on earth, when the Holy Spirit comes down upon you as the Scriptures in Matthew 4:18-19 states:

*"The Spirit of the Lord is **upon Me** (Jesus Christ), because **He has anointed Me** to preach the gospel to the poor; He has sent Me to heal the brokenhearted, to proclaim liberty to the captives and recovery of sight to the blind, to set at liberty those who are oppressed; to proclaim the acceptable year of the Lord."*

Jesus Christ was conceived by the power of the Holy Spirit and Matthew 1:18 even states, *"Now the birth of Jesus Christ was as follows: After His mother Mary was betrothed to Joseph, before they came together, she was found with **child of the Holy Spirit.**"* Jesus Christ was not only the Son of God but also the Child of the Holy Spirit. That means **the Holy Spirit was inside of Jesus Christ from His conception on**.

However, Jesus Christ did not preach one message of the Kingdom of God or perform any miracles until He was baptized by John the Baptist and the Holy Spirit came upon Him according to Matthew 3:16b, *"He saw **the Spirit of God descending** like a dove and **alighting upon Him.**"* After Jesus was led by the Spirit and tempted for forty days by the devil, He returned in the power of the Spirit to Galilee (Luke 4:14) and His ministry with kingdom authority and power began. The source and power of the ministry of Jesus on earth was the Holy Spirit. God is revealed as a triune God—three persons in one God—Father, Son, and Holy Spirit in Acts 10:38:

> "... **God** anointed **Jesus** of Nazareth with **the Holy Spirit** and power, and how he went around doing good and **healing all who were under the power of the devil**, because God was with him."

God the Father anointed Jesus the Son with the Holy Spirit. The result of the triune God in action for humanity was healing and destroying the works of the devil. This is the secret and the source of the ministry of Jesus.[32] In the same way, we must be baptized in the power of the Holy Spirit according to Acts 1:8 in order to become more than conquerors in Christ to do the work of the Kingdom of God on earth. Then we will be the Eagle Christians to go wherever the Spirit leads us to fly to expand the Kingdom of God to the ends of the earth.

We will demonstrate Christ's kingdom authority and the Holy Spirit's kingdom power to destroy the works of the devil. We are called to obey Christ's commission written in Matthew 10:7-8, 28:19-20 and Acts 1:8 until He comes back. Jesus Christ is the same yesterday, today, and forever (Hebrews 13:8) and He changes not. Jesus Christ in you would want you to do the same ministries He did while He was walking on the earth in the four gospels. Therefore, Jesus Christ who resides in you will manifest His kingdom authority to destroy the works of the devil and the Holy Spirit in you will demonstrate His kingdom power to heal the sick and cast out demons through you—God's eagle Christians.

THE SPIRIT IN US GIVES LIFE TO OUR MORTAL BODIES

The Holy Spirit in us gives life to our mortal bodies according to Romans 8:11, *"But if the Spirit of Him who raised Jesus from the dead dwells in you,* **He who raised Christ from the dead will also give life [*zoopoieo*] to your mortal bodies** *through His Spirit who dwells in you."* The Greek word for life in this Scripture *"zoopoieo"* means "come to life," "give life," "impart life," "life-giving," or "made alive." The Holy Spirit who created Jesus Christ as a human baby boy also raised Him from the dead after He was brutally tortured, abused, and received 39 lashes with a metal tip at the end of each strip of the whip.

However, when the Holy Spirit resurrected Jesus Christ from the dead, Mary Magdalene, who was the first person to encounter the risen Lord, could not recognize Him. Why? Because the Holy Spirit completely healed and removed every torture mark from His face and body, except the nail pierced hands and feet and spear that had pierced His side. The Holy Spirit gave Jesus Christ life [*zoopoieo*] from the Kingdom of Heaven not of this world. The same blessing of life has been promised to any born-again believer in Christ by the power of the Holy Spirit.

When we accept Jesus Christ as our Lord and Savior, He comes into us to release the kingdom blessings and the gift of the Holy Spirit. As the Holy Spirit dwells in us, He will impart unto us the same life [*zoopoieo*] of heaven so that we will be the carriers of the Kingdom of God on the earth to fulfill His mission for our lives. When we finish God's mission on the earth, angels (Luke 16:22) will take us to the eternal heaven so we can be with our Father and our Lord Jesus Christ forever. God will transform us by the power of the Holy Spirit to have an immortal body, just like the resurrected body of Christ. In the same manner, as the Holy Spirit indwells you, He will give life to your mortal body—including spiritual and soulish bodies. Even though you may have been born again in Christ, you may still carry spiritual scars, wounds, and a broken heart. The Holy Spirit in you will also begin to release His life [*zoopoieo*] to your wounded spiritual body to restore and heal you so that you can be a new creation in Christ.

Of course, the Holy Spirit in you can also bring life to your disease infested mortal body and heal you miraculously. Furthermore, when the Spirit of God comes into your body, He transforms you; He gives you life. There is a life in the Spirit that makes you *"free from the law of sin and death"* (Romans 8:2) and gives you holy boldness and divine personality. It is the personality of the Deity. It is God in you.[33]

Therefore, 2 Corinthians 3:17 declares, *"Now the Lord is the Spirit; and where the Spirit of the Lord is, there is liberty."* Anyone who moves in the Holy Spirit will be more than conquerors in Christ and they will be God-ordained eagle Christians to do the work of the Kingdom of God with signs, wonders, and miracles following. These final harvest eagle Christians will fly to every Unreached People Group in the world to preach the gospel of the Kingdom of God until Jesus Christ comes back.

These eagle Christians will only fly with the wind of the Holy Spirit to make the Great Commission become the Great Completion in this generation. We must be God's eagle Christians according to Isaiah 40:31, *"But those who wait on the Lord shall renew their strength;* **they shall mount up with wings like eagles***, they shall run and not be weary, they shall walk and not faint."* Eagle Christians know how to wait on the

Where Eagles Fly!

Lord to renew their strength before they launch out into His mission for the lost, suffering, and dying souls in the world.

Chapter 7

BE A VICTORIOUS FOLLOWER OF CHRIST

Jesus Christ conquered sin, sickness, curses, fear of death, and Satan at the cross and resurrected from the grave for the benefit of all of fallen humanity once and forever. He is the Conqueror, Victor, Deliverer, Healer, Provider, the King of kings and the Lord of lords. Jesus Christ declared in John 10:10, *"The thief does not come except to steal, and to kill, and to destroy. I have come that they may have life, and that they may have it more abundantly."* Therefore, it is Christ's desire for His followers to live in victorious and abundant life for His glory.

There are three Greek words for *life* used in the New Testament: ***bios, psuche,*** and ***zoe.*** These three words have different meanings, but they are all translated into English as *life*. We can identify the three different usages of the word *life* in the New Testament:

1. ***Bios*** in 1 John 2:16, *"For all that is in the world—the lust of the flesh, the lust of the eyes, and the pride of life* [physical life: ***bios***]—*is not of the Father but is of the world."* ***Bios*** refers to the life of the physical body and is where the word *biology* comes from. ***Bios*** relates to every part of human life dealing with biological and physical desires of the flesh that is directly influenced by the five senses—such as

pleasures of life in Luke 8:14. It also depicts the lifestyle of the prodigal son in Luke 15:30, *"But as soon as this son of yours came, who has devoured your livelihood (**bios**) with harlots, you killed the fatted calf for him."*

2. **Psuche** in Matthew 16:25, *"For whoever desires to save his life* [soul-life: ***psuche***] *will lose it, but whoever loses his life for My sake will find it."* **Psuche** refers to the psychological life of the human soul, that is, the mind, emotion, and will. In ***Psuche***, conscious, sub-conscious, and unconscious minds reside, and they are controlled by our free will.

   For the followers of Christ to have victorious life on the earth, they must surrender their soul-life [***psuche***] including conscious, sub-conscious, unconscious minds, and free will to the Lord and allow the mind of Christ (1 Corinthian 2:16) to govern their lives each day. Then the power of the Holy Spirit will guide their lives to all truth, whatever He hears (from Jesus Christ) He will speak to them, He will tell them things to come, He will glorify Jesus Christ through them (John 16:12-15).

3. ***Zoe*** in John 1:4, *"In Him was life* [***zoe***]*, and the life was the light of men."* **Zoe** refers to the uncreated, self-existing, eternal life of God, and the divine life uniquely possessed by the Father, Jesus Christ, and the Holy Spirit. Also, you find the same *zoe* in John 3:16, *"For God so loved the world, that He gave His only begotten Son, that whoever believes in Him shall not perish, but have eternal life* [***zoe***]*."* **Zoe** is also translated into life in John 10:10, *"I have come that*

*they may have life [**zoe**], and that they may have it more abundantly."* Therefore, when the believers in Christ pursue God ordained *zoe* to fulfill their creation mandate while living on the earth, then they will be the most fulfilled, happy, and victorious Christians.[34]

SEVEN WAYS TO WALK IN GOD'S VICTORY

We can identify the seven ways to walk in God's victorious life in Psalm 37:1-7:

*"**Do not fret** because of evildoers, nor be envious of the workers of iniquity. **Trust in the Lord**, and do good; dwell in the land, and feed on His faithfulness. **Delight yourself also in the Lord**, and He shall give you the desires of your heart. **Commit your way to the Lord**, trust also in Him, and He shall bring it to pass. He shall bring forth your righteousness as the light, and your justice as the noonday. **Rest in the Lord**, and wait patiently for Him…"*

The above Psalm will provide us with seven principles to walk in God's victorious life for His glory:

1. **Have absolute faith in God through prayers**: Whatever we are called to do for God, we must have faith in action to accomplish His will on earth. Thus, Romans 11:6 declares, *"But **without faith it is impossible to please Him**, for he who comes to God **must believe that He is**, and that **He is a rewarder of those who diligently seek Him**."* For believers in Christ to have faith in what the Holy Spirit has been guiding them to do, they must spend much time in

prayers to clearly hear His voice to understand His will, purpose, and timing to execute His plan for their lives. Without having a lifestyle of prayer each day and fasting regularly, we will not be able to have enough faith to move mountain-like problems in front of us. Believing in the Holy Spirit based on the word of God is seeing the destiny of His call in your life according to Hebrews 11:1, *"Now faith is the substance of things hoped for the evidence of things not seen."* As we have true faith in God, we will be able to believe what He promised to us through His written words, visions, dreams, prophetic proclamations, and even hearing His audible voice.

2. **Get rid of every fear, worry, and anxiety in life**: When we are fretting, worrying, or fearful about anything which is the result of the impact of dreadful circumstances unfolding in life, we often cannot think clearly and can easily fall into many traps of the devil. We will lose the situational awareness guided by the Holy Spirit and fear can lead us into a destructive path. When the King Jehoshaphat heard that the vast armies were coming against Judah, he feared, and **set himself to seek the Lord, and proclaimed a fast** throughout all Judah (2 Chronicles 20:1-18).

Jehoshaphat put his total trust in the Lord and declared in 2 Chronicles 20:6, 12, *"O Lord God of our fathers, are You not God in heaven, and **do You not rule over all the kingdoms of the nations, so that no one is able to withstand You?**" "O our God, will You not judge them? For we have no power against this great multitude that is coming against us; nor do we know what to do, **but our eyes are upon You.**"*

In the above Scriptures, we can identify that Jehoshaphat recognized his fear over the invading enemies. But **he immediately sought the Lord for help and proclaimed a fast** throughout all Judea. He acknowledged that the Lord could deliver them, and they put their eyes upon Him in faith. Then, the Lord answered Jehoshaphat's prayer and decreed in 2 Chronicles 20:17b, *"**Do not fear or be dismayed;** tomorrow go out against them, **for the Lord is with you.**"* We also need to apply the principle of Jehoshaphat's faith in God in time of our troubles so that He can fight our battles for us for His glory. We need to claim the following Scriptures when we face any fear in our lives in order to defeat the schemes of the devil:

- 2 Timothy 1:7, *"For **God has not given us a spirit of fear**, but of power and of love and of a sound mind."*
- 1 John 4:18, *"**There is no fear in love**; but perfect love casts out fear, because fear involves torment. But he who fears has not been made perfect in love."*
- Philippians 4:6-7, *"**Be anxious for nothing, but in everything by prayer and supplication, with thanks-giving**, let your requests be made known to God; and the peace of God, which surpasses all understanding, will guard your hearts and minds through Christ Jesus."*
- Isaiah 41:10, *"**Fear not**, for I am with you; be not dismayed, for I am your God. I will strengthen you, Yes, I will help you, I will uphold you with My righteous right hand."*

3. **Totally trust God with an absolute obedient heart**: Once we have total faith in God and get rid of every fear in life, then we can put our trust in Him and feed on His faithfulness according to the Scripture in Psalm 37:3, *"Trust in the Lord, and do good; dwell in the land and feed on His faithfulness."* Regardless of what our situations, circumstances, and people around us dictates, if we absolutely choose to trust God at all cost, then we can encourage ourselves in the Lord by remembering the acts of His faithfulness in the past.

   However, our trust in the Lord must be implemented by an obedient heart to follow His instructions and directions regardless of how they may not make sense to us at that moment or circumstance. **Because obedience is the only key to unlock the blessings and favor of God in our lives.**

4. **Delight yourself in the Lord by praising Him at all circumstances:** Delight means a high degree of gratification or pleasure. It is easy for us to delight ourselves in the Lord when things are going very well in life, but not so when our circumstances are in a very difficult place. The devil wants us to be depressed, oppressed, complaining, and despondent when it seems as though all things are going against our wishes even though we prayed about them with all our hearts.

   However, the Lord wants us to give Him all the glory and praise whether our circumstances are preferable or undesirable. We can read in Hebrews 13:15, *"Therefore by Him let us continually offer **the sacrifice of praise to God**, that is, the fruit of our lips, giving thanks to His name."* When we delight ourselves in the Lord by giving Him the sacrifice of praise with a grateful heart, then He is very pleased with us and will give us our heart's desires in His perfect timing.

I believe that God gave the desires of my heart to continuously serve Him by supernaturally healing me in four days after the accident, when I praised and delighted myself in Him regardless of the excruciating pain in my back. When we do that, then the devil will not have any victory over our lives because we delight ourselves in the Lord no matter what happens in life.

5. **Commit your ways to the Lord:** Commit in Hebrew is *galal* which means roll down or roll away or take away. That means God wants you to roll all your ways, thoughts, logics, burdens, fears, insecurities, and commitments down unto Him with absolutely trust in His ways, then He will bring them to pass according to His perfect plan and time.

The Lord declares in Psalm 55:8-9, 11, *"For **My thoughts are not your thoughts, nor are your ways My ways**," says the Lord. "For as the heavens are higher than the earth, so are My ways higher than your ways, and My thoughts than your thoughts. **So shall My word be that goes forth from My mouth; It shall not return to Me void, but it shall accomplish what I please**, and it shall prosper in the thing for which I sent it."* Therefore, we can absolutely trust the Lord and His divine instructions for our lives. We simply need to obey and accomplish them for His glory.

6. **Rest in the Lord:** Once we follow the above five steps wholeheartedly, then we enter into His divine rest. In Hebrews 4:1-3a reiterates about entering His rest, *"Therefore, since a promise remains of entering His rest, let us fear lest any of you seem to have come short of it. For indeed the gospel was preached to us as well as to them; but* **the word which they heard did not profit them, not being mixed with faith** *in those who heard it.* **For we who have believed do enter that rest***..."*

   As we enter God's rest in dealing with every kind of life matter, we are trusting Him to handle them according to His perfect will and time. Resting in God does not mean that we do not do anything to accomplish His direction in life, but we must faithfully follow the above five steps each day. Then we need to wait patiently for God to act on behalf of our prayers by not worrying or fretting, regardless of how the devil is trying to buffet against us so as not to obey or follow or be still in Him until He moves.

7. **Enjoy God's beauty of holiness:** Only when we truly enter God's divine rest, can we begin to experience His beauty of holiness. We will not be conformed to this world, but be transformed by the renewing of our minds, that we may prove what is that good and acceptable and perfect will of God (Romans12:2). As we worship the Lord in His beauty of holiness, all the affairs of this world will become strangely dim and all our worries and fears will dissipate under the glory of God. We can boldly proclaim Psalm 96:1-3, 9, *"Oh, sing to the Lord a new song! Sing to the Lord, all the earth. Sing to the Lord, bless His name; proclaim the*

good news of His salvation from day to day. Declare His glory among the nations, His wonders among all peoples…Oh, worship the *Lord in the beauty of holiness!*" Then we can truly live victorious Christian lives as more than conquerors and as His divine eagle Christians. If God is for us, who can be against us? No weapon formed against us shall prosper all the days of our lives.

LIVE ACCORDING TO THE REALITY OF JOHN 14:20-21

Jesus Christ declared in John 14:20-21, *"At that day you will know that **I am in My Father, and you in Me, and I in you**. He who has My commandments and keeps them, it is he who loves Me. And he who loves Me will be loved by My Father, and **I will love him and manifest Myself to him**."* "*At that day*" in the above Scripture, Jesus Christ was speaking about the day of Pentecost when His 120 followers in the upper room in Jerusalem (Acts 1:14-15) were baptized with the Promise of the Father—the Holy Spirit. Then, Jesus Christ stated in Acts 1:5, *"for John truly baptized with water, but **you shall be baptized with the Holy Spirit** not many days from now."*

Furthermore, Jesus Christ clearly declared the purpose of the baptism of the Holy Spirit and His Great Commission in Acts 1:8, *"But **you shall receive power when the Holy Spirit has come upon you**; and **you shall be witnesses to Me** in Jerusalem, and in all Judea and Samaria, and **to the end of the earth**."* The wrong focus of the baptism of the Holy Spirit has been solely identifying with speaking in unknown tongues. Of course, it is important to speak in tongues if we are baptized in the Holy Spirit. But the main purpose of the baptism in the Holy Spirit is to receive His power to make the Great Commission become the Great Completion in this generation to fulfill the charge of Christ to His followers in Matthew 24:14, *"And **this gospel of the kingdom will be preached in all the world as a witness to all the nations, and then the end will come."*** According to the above Scripture, Jesus Christ will only come back when the last unreached people group will hear the gospel of the kingdom. Then the end will come.

Therefore, the vision of the Father for sending His only begotten Son, Jesus Christ to the earth is to accomplish His deliverance plan for the fallen mankind from every people, tongue, tribe, and nation to be saved. For the followers of Christ to accomplish the Great Commission, they needed to be filled with the authority of Jesus Christ (Matthew 28:18) and the power of the Holy Spirit to destroy the works of the devil according to 1 John 3:8b, *"For this purpose the Son of God was manifested, that **He might destroy the works of the devil.**"*

So, we can say that the daily mission of God for any believer in Christ is to accomplish His command in Matthew 10:7-8, *"And **as you go, preach,** saying, **'The kingdom of heaven is at hand. Heal the sick, cleanse the lepers, raise the dead, cast out demons.** Freely you have received, freely give.'"* What have we freely received as followers of Christ? The answer is the baptism in the Holy Spirit to move in His power to destroy the works of the devil in our own Jerusalem and to the end of the earth. To appropriate that, we need to fully understand the power of John 14:20-21 to live as God's victorious eagle Christians to fulfill His creation mandate for our lives each day. Jesus Christ knew that His disciples could not do the works of Him without releasing His authority and the power of the Holy Spirit to them. Therefore, Jesus Christ was replicating His divine relationship with the Father that caused Him to accomplish Father God's supernatural works of the Kingdom of God on the earth with His followers. Once we understand the power of John 14:20-21, we will experience the manifestation of Christ in our lives and ministries for His glory as it was promised in John 14:21, *"He who has My commandments and keeps them, it is he who loves Me. And he who loves Me will be loved by My Father, and **I will love him and manifest Myself to him**."*

Let's unfold the power of John 14:20 together: *"At that day* (the day of Pentecost) *you will know that I am in My Father* (because He was already ascended to heaven), *and you in Me* (if we are literally in Christ, then we are in the Kingdom of heaven with Him) *and I in you* (the King of kings of the heavens and the earth indwell us)."* Therefore, if we are in Christ, then positionally speaking, we are already in the heavenly places in Christ according to Ephesians 2:5-6, *"even when we were dead in trespasses, made us alive together with Christ (by grace you have been saved), and raised us up together and **made us sit together in the heavenly places in Christ Jesus**."*

So, we can declare that **we do not work for God, but from God**—appropriating all His glory, authority, power, resources, blessings, and anointing to do His kingdom work according to His perfect will on earth. If we reside inside of Christ in heavenly place, then it is a Satan free zone, a sin free zone, a sickness free zone, a curse free zone, and a fear of death free zone. Thus, we can freely declare Romans 8:1, *"There is **therefore now no condemnation to those who are in Christ Jesus**, who do not walk according to the flesh, but according to the Spirit."*

If we live inside of Christ, we will naturally walk in the Spirit because Christ always walks according to the Spirit. Or the other way around, if Jesus Christ is in us, then the King of the Kingdom of Heaven is within us to fulfill the prophetic word of Luke 17:21b, *"For indeed, the kingdom of God is within you."* Then, **the believers in Christ are the carriers of the Kingdom of God on the earth** with the authority of Christ and the power of the Holy Spirit to do the will of the Father God—**making the Great Commission become the Great Completion in this generation**.

As we fully understand the power of John 14:20-21, we can be more than conquerors in Christ to live victorious lives for His glory on the earth. We can identify that Jesus Christ was replicating His perfect relationship with the Father with the sons and daughters of God to do the work on the earth as He did in John 9b-11, *"He who has seen Me has seen the Father...Do you not believe that **I am in the Father, and the Father in Me**? The words that I speak to you I do not speak on My own authority; but **the Father who dwells in Me does the works**. Believe Me that **I am in the Father and the Father in Me**, or else believe Me for the sake of the works themselves."*

According to the above Scriptures, we can identify that it was the Father, who indwelled Jesus Christ, who did all the supernatural works for His glory. Therefore, Jesus Christ was giving all the credits of His works on earth to the Father who did them through Him. Ultimately, Jesus Christ wants us to have the same relationship with Him by allowing us to be in Him and He in us. Now we can see that we can do the same works that Christ did and even greater things for His glory **because it is Christ who does all the works of the Kingdom of God through us**. Once we truly embrace the power of John 14:20-21, we can tangibly live Christ's victorious life on earth as His eagle Christians by flying wherever the wind of the Holy Spirit carries us to go with the authority and power of God.

OVERCOMING THE TRIAL

In April 2022, my one and only wife, Margarita was diagnosed as having a very severe aortic stenosis in her heart's main valve. Her cardiologist told her that she would have to go through the Transcatheter Aortic Valve Replacement (TAVR) surgery within six months because her main valve was only opening one centimeter (the normal heart valve opens three centimeters) and not fully closing.

Margarita's doctor told her that she may only live up to six months without the surgery because her heart was functioning 30 percent capacity in April. I was invited to minister in the Netherlands in the latter part of July to the beginning of August. We began to pray and ask the Lord to have mercy on Margarita. We sincerely petitioned to the Lord to either supernaturally recreate Margarita's main valve or find the best heart surgeon to perform the TAVR procedure on her so that she would not die but live to fulfill her God ordained creation mandate for His glory.

By the grace of God, she was accepted by one of the best heart surgeons in America to do her surgery on July 22. However, I was very much concerned about Margarita's serious condition. In the beginning of July, she was not able to do any normal functions and even had a very difficult time of walking from the bedroom to the living room. She could hardly breathe after walking a few steps. Therefore, I had to do everything for her, and I did so with joy. She was scheduled to have the TAVR surgery on the morning of July 22nd. However, her condition was rapidly deteriorating since July 1st. There was fear in our hearts that Margarita might not make it until the 22nd. Of course, the devil was whispering in her ears that she would die. Therefore, Margarita and I decided to praise the Lord no matter what fears the devil was trying to instill in our hearts. As we kept praising the Lord and did Communion each morning, we were able to fix our eyes on Him and not on the source of fear. When God's presence and light surrounded us by rendering our sacrifice of praises as often as we could, His glory expelled all our fears and gave us His assurance that Margarita will live and not die (Psalm 118:17).

Also, the Holy Spirit assured us that He would heal Margarita according to His promise in Jeremiah 30:17, *"For I will restore health to you and heal you of your wounds, says the Lord."* Even though Margarita's condition was getting worse each day as we patiently waiting for her surgery date on the 22nd, we were determined to trust His promise in Romans 8:11 as well, *"But if the Spirit of Him who raised Jesus from the dead dwells in you,* **He who raised Christ from the dead will also give life to your mortal bodies** *through His Spirit who dwells in you."*

Finally, I took Margarita to the Norfolk Heart Center at 5:00 a.m. on July 22nd and they did all the necessary tests and an EKG to prepare for the surgery. She went into the surgery at around 11:30 a.m. and she came to the recovery room at 1:30 p.m. after her surgery was successfully done. Shortly after that, I was able to go into the room and prayed with Margarita. We gave all the glory to the Lord and praised Him for giving her a second chance at life to finish the race well for His glory. She was discharged the next day at around 11:30 a.m. In the meantime, I was scheduled to minister at a conference in the Netherlands from July 25th to August 3rd. Before Margarita went to the surgery, we sincerely prayed to know the will of God for the mission trip. We needed to know if I should stay at home, or if it was God's will for me to go to the conference as one of the main speakers. As we prayed, Margarita and I received God's answer that I should go and minister at the conference. Especially, Margarita insisted that I should go and save souls during the conference for young people so that the devil would not have victory over our lives. In the meantime, my son and daughter-in-law would come down and take care of Margarita. As my son's family came down and began to take care of her, I felt God's peace to go and minister at the conference.

During the conference in the Netherlands, the devil tried all different ways to block me from ministering with kingdom authority and power because the leaders of the conference were from the churches that did not believe in the move and power of the Holy Spirit. Regardless of the opposition by the leaders, I was able to minister to teenagers and young adult groups of over 100 people and more than 70 of them gave their lives to Christ during the altar calls. I gave all the glory to the Lord for 70 plus souls who had chosen to enter the Kingdom of God during the conference.

Whatever the devil tried to hinder the work of the Kingdom of God in our lives, we had decided to trust the Lord with all our hearts by giving all the glory to Him with thanksgiving in our hearts. God gave us His victory in Margarita's healing and saving souls in the conference. We can claim Romans 8:28 with total confidence in Christ, *"And we know that all things work together for good to those who love God, to those who are the called according to His purpose."* **"If God is for us, who can be against us?"** (Romans 8:31b)

Chapter 8

MOUNT UP WITH WINGS LIKE EAGLES

We are called to be Eagle Christians for God's glory. Eagles are heaven bound—always soaring up high toward the sky. Chickens are always earth bound—their eyes are constantly looking down to the ground searching for the grains. Chickens are very territorial in nature and they will peck other chickens away if their little space has been invaded by others. In this last chapter, we will discover the characteristics of eagles versus chickens to conclude that if we are in Christ, we are called to be His eagle Christians to fulfill His divine vision, mission, and action plans while we live on the earth.

Jesus Christ proclaimed in John 16:33, *"These things I have spoken to you, that in Me you may have peace.* ***In the world you will have tribulation; but be of good cheer, I have overcome the world.****"* How can we overcome the world when tribulation comes to our lives? God never promises that His children will not go through the tribulations in this life, but He assures them that He will be with them according to Isaiah 43:1-2:

> *"But now thus says the Lord, who created you, O Jacob, and He who formed you, O Israel:* ***'Fear not, for I have redeemed you; I have called you by your name; you are Mine****. When you pass through the waters,* ***I will be with you****; and through the rivers, they*

shall not overflow you. When you walk through the fire, you shall not be burned, nor shall the flame scorch you.'" If we are in Christ, He has redeemed us and called us by our names because we belong to Him. God is calling us not to fear when we go through the tribulations like the waters, the rivers, and even the fire because He will be with us through the painful journeys of sufferings in this life. There are three types of tribulations that the children of God may go through in life:

1) **Devil induced**: We can fall into the devil's traps by not seeking the Lord's guidance and willfully choosing to fall into the temptations. He only comes to us to steal, and to kill, and to destroy what God has ordained for us to enjoy—His divine purpose, plan, and life on the earth.

2) **Self-induced**: We can blindly follow our own ways to fulfill our desires, will, the lust of eyes, the lust of the flesh, and the pride of life. "*I did it my way*" can lead us into many sorrows and tribulations in life.

3) **God allowed**: God may allow the tribulation to come into our lives so He can test us to know what is in our hearts. God declared in Deuteronomy 8:2, "*And you shall remember that the Lord your God led you all the way these forty years in the wilderness,* **to humble you and test you, to know what was in your heart,** *whether you would keep His commandments or not.*"

One way or another, the children of God will be faced with all three situations in life, where we get to make the choice who we will serve, the devil, the flesh, or the Lord. When we choose to sin, and as Romans 3:23 states, *"for all have sinned and **fall short of the glory of God**."* We fall short of His glory—losing His presence, anointing, favor, blessings, and divine peace. At those times, we need to repent of our wicked ways and return to God's divine purpose, plan, and creation mandate to fulfill His will in our lives for His glory.

Once we wholeheartedly return to God, then His glory will be restored with His divine peace permeating into all aspects of the journeys of our short lives on the earth. This happens when we put our total trust in the Lord and follow Him to fulfill His missions in our lives for His glory. Even though we may fall short of the glory of God at times, we can rise up again and turn back to Him as His eagle Christians to soar up high by the wind of the Holy Spirit to fly to the destiny where He establishes for us.

EARTH-BOUND CHICKEN CHRISTIANS

- **Chickens easily follow any leader without knowing where he is leading them**: They live to please the leader at all costs to receive his favor and recognition in front of others. They are also people pleasers and organize the ministries based on the demands of the people. They are great spectators who want to take part in the events without having to commit any responsibilities. After the events are over, they love to make their own critiques about those who worked very hard to make them happen. They are very opinionated in all matters of the church without offering their efforts and time to make them better. They are gossipers, talebearers, and love to create rumors about anyone or any matters.

- **Chickens love to take credits for any contribution**: They love to blow a small matter out of the proportion if it is dealing with gaining any recognition in the church. If anyone else is trying to take credit for what they have contributed, they are not afraid to create false narratives to discredit them. Just like if a chicken finds a worm or a bug in the dirt, they all want it at all costs. They will come and attack the one who found it to take away his worm so they can claim it for their own achievement.

- **Chickens are insecure and fearful**: They will not allow any other one to rise above their anointed levels of ministries and if anyone does so, then they will be quick to demote or eliminate them to secure their own position of authority. They love to steal other chicken's property to make it their own achievement. They are constantly borrowing the ideas of other successful ministries to improve their own without first consulting with the Lord in prayers. When they fail, they will blame others and always provide excuses for their mistakes. They will never acknowledge their failures or apologize their shortcomings before the congregation. They are cowards and when they are cornered by others, they will run away without taking any responsibilities.

- **Chickens are earth-bound and not interested in the move of the Holy Spirit:** They are happy to be inside of the coop and seldom they want to fly outside of the cage to explore the rest of the world. They would rather be bound by the denominational doctrines made by men than allow the move of the Holy Spirit to transform the religious-spirit controlled dead church. They will rather honor their traditions than the fresh move of the Spirit to bring revivals in their churches. Their eyes are focused only on the earth to find their next food. They would love to control every aspect of their church ministries by creating many man-made programs rather than allow the Holy Spirit to move in His own power to deliver the people from bondages. They have the spirits of Pharisees and desire to crucify the move of the resurrected Lord Jesus Christ and the anointing of the Holy Spirit. They become the frozen-chosen Christians without ever flying above to see the whole scope of God for their ministries.

- **Chickens have a form of godliness but denying its power:** The bible describes very clearly how the chicken Christians would behave in the latter days in 2 Timothy 3:1-5, *"But know this, that in the last days perilous times will come: For men will be lovers of themselves, lovers of money, boasters, proud, blasphemers, disobedient to parents, unthankful, unholy, unloving, unforgiving, slanderers, without self-control, brutal, despisers of good, traitors, headstrong, haughty, lovers of pleasure rather than lovers of God, having a form of godliness but denying its power. And from such people turn away!"*

- **Chickens will also twist the truth of God**: They will replace, in the name of love, what is the truth of God with secular humanistic ideas. But the word of God in 1 Corinthians 6:9-10 declares, **"Do you not know that the unrighteous will not inherit the kingdom of God?** *Do not be deceived. Neither fornicators, nor idolaters,* *nor adulterers, nor homosexuals, nor sodomites, nor thieves, nor covetous, nor drunkards, nor revilers, nor extortioners will inherit the kingdom of God."* If we are truly born-again sons and daughters of God, we must promote and preach the true message of the Kingdom of God without wavering by the pressure of the worldly humanistic ideals of men.

- **Chickens are only interested in building their own kingdom:** Unfortunately, they are more about building their own kingdom and campuses on the earth than evangelizing lost souls by expanding the Kingdom of God to fulfill the Great Commission become the Great Completion in this generation. They will compromise in whatever the ways necessary to keep their people inside the coop and to bring other chickens into it by preaching watered-down and ear-tickling messages of their own kingdom.

    The move of the Holy Spirit will always be controlled for the sake of keeping their program-based time schedules in the church. They will play secular music during the Christian holidays to draw secular people into their earthly kingdom. They will make any salvation calls in Christ to be the most comfortable and non-threatening ways to unbelievers because they are not truly interested in transforming them to be powerful disciples of Christ but rather to join the church and become members. They are creating the uniformly shaped bricks made by religious denominational spirits to satisfy the tradition of the church instead of creating the living stones to fulfill the word of God by the power of the Holy Spirit.

Where Eagles Fly!

BE A HEAVEN-BOUND EAGLE CHRISTIAN

According to an article by Wildlife Informer, eagles are large birds of prey, with powerful hooked beaks and sharp talons. They are superb flyers and can reach speeds of over 93 mph (150 km/h). Eagles have incredible eyesight that allows them to see prey from great distances. Their eyes are four to eight times sharper than a human's, and they can spot a rabbit or squirrel from up to two miles away.[35] Parrots are very talkative but cannot fly high. In contrast, eagles are normally silent but has a God ordained instinct to touch the sky. As we examine the unique characteristics of eagles, we will also be able to learn from them how to become God's eagle Christians to fly high to fulfill His creation mandate in our lives for His glory.

1. **Eagles have extraordinary vision**: Eagles can lock on a prey as far away as three miles away. Once they put their focus on the prey, they will not alter the course regardless of the obstacles until they capture it. When eagles are searching for prey from the nest, their eyes are constantly sweeping out the horizon to identify prey with their laser guided eye-vision. Once they are on their mission to capture the prey, they will stealthily fly as quickly as possible to come upon it. However, before they launch their effort to catch the prey, they patiently wait for the perfect timing to execute their mission.

Therefore, we, the eagle Christians, require God's wide and divine vision for our lives to fulfill His mission whenever and wherever we may be called to go. We must follow the biblical instruction in Isaiah 40:31, "*But* ***those who wait on the Lord*** *shall renew their strength;* ***they shall mount up with*** *wings like eagles, they shall run and not be weary, they shall walk and not faint."* In order for us to succeed in our God ordained missions in life, we must learn to wait upon His perfect time to move and act upon what He has instructed us to accomplish.

We also need to understand the overarching vision of God for the fallen world. **The main vision of God for the world is to make the Great Commission become the Great Completion in this generation** according to Acts 1:8, Matthew 28:18-20, Mark 16:17-20, and Matthew 24:14. Eagle Christian churches must engage in fulfilling the Great Commission by sending their missions mobilizers to equip indigenous missionaries to evangelize the Unreached People Groups (UPGs) adjacent to their regions. They can also support other missions groups which have been engaging in evangelizing the UPGs in the world.

Eagles Christians are not just called to become members of a church to warm the pews each Sunday, but to be engaged in doing God's overall vision for the world. So that someday soon, God's prophetic words in Revelations 7:9-10 can be fulfilled in this generation, *"After these things I looked, and behold,* ***a great multitude which no one could number, of all nations, tribes, peoples, and tongues, standing before the throne and before the Lamb****, clothed with white robes, with palm branches in their hands, and crying out with a loud voice, saying, 'Salvation belongs to our God who sits on the throne, and to the Lamb!'"*

Then **what is the mission of God for the world**? The mission of God is to make disciples of Christ and not just converts, so that they can be His eagle Christians to fly high to accomplish their creation mandate on the earth. Jesus Christ commands eagle Christians to make disciples in Matthew 28:19, *"Go therefore and* ***make disciples of all the nations****,* *baptizing them in the name of the Father and of the Son and of the Holy Spirit."* The greatest problem of any pastors and church leaders are currently dealing with is over 80 percent of the congregation who are not willing to be engaged in doing God's kingdom works but simply attend the services each Sunday.

They are simply church members and not true disciples of Christ to be His eagle Christians. Many of them believe that they are not called to do the ministry of winning the souls and making disciples, because they are not one of the trained leaders at the church. Biblical educations and degrees, though they are important to equip leaders, are not the qualifiers for the workers for God's kingdom. The baptism and anointing in the Holy Spirit will equip any eagle Christian to be His minister. God has not called the followers of Christ to only fill the church, but to fill the earth with eagle Christians.

What is the action plan of God for the fallen souls in the world? His action plans are for His eagle Christians to preach the Kingdom of God wherever they go each day to lost souls and to destroy the works of the devil by delivering them from every yoke of bondage. Therefore, Jesus Christ commissions His eagle Christians to obey His commandment in Matthew 10:7-8, *"And **as you go, preach**, saying, the kingdom of heaven is at hand. **Heal the sick**, cleanse the lepers, raise the dead, **cast out demons**. Freely you have received, freely give."*

We can identify three main calls of Christ for eagle Christians: 1) preach the Kingdom of Heaven; 2) heal the sick; 3) cast out demons. Nowadays, many Western churches do not exercise any of the above commandments during their Sunday services because they are afraid of losing their members or newcomers in case they will be disturbed by the Holy Spirit moving in His power with signs, wonders, and miracles cfollowing. When the Spirit moves, He will definitely disturb our man-made religious programs that have no power thereof. The service will not be able to keep the orders of having four worship songs, 5 to 10 minutes of announcements, a 5-minute speech to arouse the congregation to give tithes and offerings, and 30-minute sermons with few altar calls to give an opportunity for anyone to accept Jesus Christ as their Lord and Savior.

If they do any altar calls, they will do in such a way that the recipients will not be recognized to protect their privacy and normally do not mention anything about repenting of their sins. Even though Jesus Christ died on the cross naked, humiliated publicly, and suffered tremendously for our sins, most churches have the salvation call demonstrate minimum commitment and transformation by the new believers. Meanwhile, Jesus Christ declares in 1 John 3:8b, *"For this purpose the Son of God was manifested, that* **He might destroy the works of the devil.***"*

Many people may come to a church each Sunday, but they may be still totally bound by the bondages or addictions of the devil. There are very few ministers in the Western church who are anointed and trained to deliver these so-called Christian church goers who are remaining in many different forms of bondage, addiction, depression, oppression, and even demonization.

If we examine the Book of Acts, we can clearly witness that not only the Apostles, but every believer moved in the power of the Holy Spirit to save lost souls and destroy the works of the devil in their lives. In this last hour of the Last Days, we need to become God's eagle Christians to fly high by the wind of the Holy Spirit to save as many souls as we can by destroying the works of the devil with signs, wonders, and miracles following.

2. **Eagles normally fly alone at high altitude**: Eagles do not fly with other earth bound and self-centered small birds but only with other likeminded heaven-bound other eagles. Likewise, we the eagle Christians also need to avoid flying alongside of narrow-minded, negative, self-centered, proud, egotistic, pessimistic, complaining, and critical people. Eagle Christians must fly with other eagles such as like-minded, Sprit-filled, generous, kind, optimistic, encouraging, loving, obedient, and tenacious sons and daughters of God.[36]

There is an idiom saying that "birds of a feather, flock together." It suggests that if you want to know what a person is like, examine his or her friends. Also, people with similar background or education have a lot in common or the same attitudes, and stick together. Therefore, eagle Christians must fly among anointed, Spirit filled, wise, loving, kind, and yet tenacious and fearless other eagles to achieve their God ordained mission in life.

There are several warnings in the Bible about associating with evil or bad company. We read in 1 Corinthians 15:33, *"Do not be deceived: 'Evil company corrupts good habits.'"* Proverbs 13:20, *"He who walks with wise men will be wise, but the companion of fools will be destroyed."* In Amos 3:3 states, *"Can two walk together, unless they are agreed?"* The Psalmist declares in Psalm119:63, *"I am a companion of all who fear You, and of those who keep Your precepts."*

For eagle Christians to accomplish God ordained missions in life, they must find like-minded eagles to fly together in unity to maximize their time to obtain the best outcome for His glory. Thus, the Apostle Paul pleads with the disciples in the Corinthian church in 1 Corinthians 1:10, *"Now I plead with you, brethren, by the name of our Lord Jesus Christ, that you all speak the same thing, and that there is no divisions among you, but that you be perfectly joined together in the same mind and in the same judgment."* When eagle Christians fly together with other eagles with the same feathers, they will find the unity in the Spirit to accomplish what God asks them to do with excellent results.

3. **Eagles are bold and very courageous**: Once eagles fix their eyes on a prey, they are very courageous to catch it no matter what the challenge or threats they may face in due course. Eagles are stealthy during the pursuit of the prey and come upon one utilizing surprise tactics and overpowering power. Eagles never give up or surrender to the adversities of life. If they fail in their first attempt to catch a prey, they will find another opportunity to capture the next one or another one after until they are successful.

Therefore, the eagle Christians must be fearless and tenacious in all circumstances, situations, and people around them regardless of their threats, oppositions, or blatant attacks instigated by the power of darkness. Eagles are not afraid of the storm but they face it head on because it will lift them up high above the storm cloud decks to glide in the wind of adversity to reach their destiny without any fear. In contrast, when a storm comes, all other birds will try to hide in trees or any other safe place that they can find. Therefore, eagle Christians must not be afraid of the storms that come into our lives, but we need to soar up high with the wind of the Holy Spirit to rise above the storm to reach our God ordained destiny for His glory. Eagle Christians need to put their total faith in the Lord and follow His advice in the word of God:

- 2 Timothy 1:7, *"For God has not given us a spirit of fear,* ***but of power and of love and of a sound mind."***

- 1 John 4:18, *"There is no fear in love; but **perfect love casts out fear**, because fear involves torment. But he who fears has not been made perfect in love."*
- Isaiah 41:10, *"**Fear not, for I am with you**; be not dismayed, for I am your God. I will strengthen you, yes, I will help you, I will uphold you with my righteous right hand."*
- Deuteronomy 31:6, *"**Be strong and of good courage**, do not fear nor be afraid of them; for **the Lord your God, He is the One who goes with you**. He will not leave you nor forsake you."*
- Psalm 23:4, *"Yea, though I walk through the valley of the shadow of death, **I will fear no evil; for You are with me**; Your rod and Your staff, they comfort me."*

Even though eagle Christians may go through some of the most difficult things in life such as the sickness, debilitating accidents, loss of a loved one, financial collapse, natural disasters, famine, or war, we must not quit, give up, or surrender our will to fight the enemy. Regardless of what eagle Christians face in life, they are fearless and tenacious to put their total faith in the Lord and will declare the victory in Jesus Christ by declaring Romans 8:31-35, 37-39:

> *"What then shall we say to these things? **If God is for us, who can be against us**? He who did not spare His own Son, but delivered Him up for us all, how shall He not with Him also freely give us all things? **Who shall bring a charge against God's elect? It is God who justifies**. Who is he who condemns? It is Christ who dies, and furthermore is also risen, who is even at the right hand of God, who also makes intercession for us. Who shall separate us from the love of Christ? Shall*

tribulation, or distress, or persecution, or famine, or nakedness, or peril, or sword? **Yet in all these things we are more than conquerors through Him who loved us.** *For I am persuaded that* **neither death nor life, nor angels nor principalities nor powers, nor things present nor things to come, nor height nor depth, nor any other created thing, shall be able to separate us from the love of God which in in Christ Jesus our Lord.***"*

I met a Ukrainian refugee lady with two beautiful children in a refugee center in Krakow, Poland in May 2022. I asked her what had happened to her and how she escaped from Bucha, Ukraine. She told me that Russian soldiers came into her town and began to torture and kill any men they randomly found, and they also raped and killed many young girls and women in her town.

They killed her husband in front of her home, so after the Russian soldiers passed by her home, she quietly came out and carried her husband's dead body into her back yard and buried him that night. Afterwards, she packed one bag and left the town in the night with her two children. It took over 56 hours to arrive at the Polish border. Polish people were very kind, and they gave a stroller and toys to her children.

Eventually, they arranged for her to be at the refugee center which was operated by a Christian pastor. While I was hearing her story, I had to hold back my tears. She was an Orthodox believer who did not know the gift of eternal life in Christ. So, I was able to explain the salvation message of Christ to her and she accepted Jesus Christ as her Lord and Savior. Then, she told me that she could feel the peace of God coming down upon her and she said to me, *"Now I want to live for Jesus Christ and for my children. I will not allow the evil*

Russian soldiers to ruin my life anymore. Thank you for leading me to Christ!" I believe that she became an eagle Christian. Regardless of what had happened to her, I was able to see in her eyes the love of Christ and the will to survive no matter what the devil had done to her husband and her family. She was more than a conqueror in Christ. During that mission trip, I was able to lead many Ukrainian refugees to the Lord in Poland, organize some relief goods to be given them, and send some relief aid to struggling Ukrainian refugees in Ukraine.

    4. **Eagles have God ordained wings with special feathers:** Eagles have very large wing spans. The average wingspan of a female Bald Eagle is approximately 86.4" (7.2 feet). To add to this, they have feathers that are specially adapted to help them fly. The composition of their feathers is very light but also very strong. This allows them to soar through the air with ease and gives them the power to dive at high speeds when hunting.

    Therefore, three noteworthy parts of eagles are their extraordinary vision to lock on a prey, their enormous wings with agility to fly stealthily toward their target, and their very powerful talons to snatch one into the air to their nest. Thus, eagles groom and maintain their wings meticulously so that they can be ready to soar up high whenever they need.[37]

    Likewise, eagle Christians must spend quality time in developing their God given vision to fulfill His mission in their lives by reading the word of God daily, praying without ceasing, and having constant fellowship with the Holy Spirit. We must be ready to soar up high like eagles to engage in God's mission to save lost souls, to heal the sick, and to deliver anyone who has been suffering under the bondages of demons as the Scripture in 2 Timothy 4:2 instructs us, *"Preach the word! Be ready in season and out of season. Convince, rebuke, exhort, with all long-suffering and teaching.*" Eagle Christians are also commanded to engage in Matthew 10:7-8 by the Lord Jesus Christ, "*And as you go, preach, saying, 'The kingdom of heaven is at hand. Heal the sick, cleanse the lepers, raise the dead, cast out demons. Freely you have received, freely give.'*"

Sons and daughters of God are not called to be chicken Christians but eagle Christians. Chickens are always earth-bound but eagle Christians are heaven-bound to soar up high to conquer their promise land each day for His glory. Eagle Christians must take good care of our God ordained spiritual wings in order to fly—constantly praying in the Spirit to hear His still small voice to engage in His divine mission on earth to destroy the works of the devil and rescue those who are under the bondages of darkness.

5. **Eagles are very protective of their offsprings**: God compares Himself to that of a mother eagle who spreads her wings to cover her young and carry them away from any danger in Exodus 19:4, "*You have seen what I did to the Egyptians. You know how **I carried you on eagles' wings and brought you to Myself.**"* God describes Himself in a similar way in Deuteronomy 32:11, "*As an eagle stirs up its nest, hovers over its young, spreading out its wings, taking them up, carrying them on its wings.*"

In order for eagle Christians to be protected by the Lord and be carried by His mighty wings, we need to obey His instructions and commandments described in Deuteronomy 28:1-2, "*Now it shall come to pass, **if you diligently obey the voice of the LORD your God**, to observe carefully all His commandments which I command you today, that the LORD your God will set you high above all nations of the earth. And **all these blessings shall come upon you and overtake you, because you obey the voice of the LORD your God.**"* Then the promise of God in Psalm 91:1, 3-4, will be fulfilled in their lives: *"He who dwells in the secret place of the Most High shall abide under the shadow of the Almighty...Surely He shall deliver you from the snare of the Fowler and from the perilous pestilence. He shall cover you with His feathers, **and under His wing you shall take refuge**; His truth shall be your shield and buckler."*

Once we have God's divine protection under His wings, then we also need to protect our spiritual flocks at all cost from the power of darkness and temptations of the devil. We need to disciple new converts to be walking in the ways of the Holy Spirit in holiness and purity. Mature eagle Christians must train and equip new followers of Christ to stay together in flying formation to soar up high to not only see the vision of God for their lives but also understand God's divine purpose and plan for themselves. Eagle Christian leaders must feed and tend God's children just like mother eagles take care of and protect their offsprings.

6. **Eagles make their nest on high**: Eagles do not build their nests on any low ground and earth-bound locations, but on very high cliffs where other predators cannot reach them easily. Sitting up on a high nest on the cliff, eagles spy out the prey with their super vision as described in Job 39:27-29, *"Does the eagle mount up at your command, and make its nest on high? On the rock it dwells and resides, on the crag of the rock and the stronghold. From there it spies out the prey; its eyes observe from afar."*

Likewise, eagle Christians must put their dwelling places in heavenly realms so as to be closer to the presence and glory of God and to observe the tactics of the enemy on a spiritually high ground. Therefore, Ephesians 1:3 declares, *"Blessed be the God and Father of our Lord Jesus Christ, who has blessed* us with every spiritual blessing in the heavenly places in Christ." Truly, our citizenship is in heaven according to Philippians 3:20, *"For our citizenship is in heaven, from which we also eagerly wait for the Savior, the Lord Jesus Christ."* Eagle Christians must not be earthly but be heavenly minded by surrendering our conscious, sub-conscious, and unconscious minds unto the Lord and be guided by the mind of Christ.

Thus, 1 Corinthians 2:16 states, *"For 'who has known the mind of the LORD that he may instruct Him?' But **we have the mind of Christ**."* If we are in Christ, His heavenly mind will control every thought in our minds and hearts in Him to do the will of the Father on earth as it is in heaven. Chicken Christians dwell in their earthly coops because they are totally earthly minded, but eagle Christians build their spiritual nests in heavenly realms to carry out God's mission on earth by working from God and His all authority and power in heaven and on earth.

7. Eagles catch the current of the wind to soar up high: Eagles are not afraid of any storm rising on the horizon, because they can soar up higher above it. The stronger the wind, the higher eagles can soar by allowing the current to carry them up to the sky. We the eagle Christians also allow the wind of the Holy Spirit to carry us to the spiritually higher ground each day by praying in the Spirit, meditating on the word of God, and doing what He has called and ordained us to do.

John 3:8 declares, *"The wind blows where it wishes, and you hear the sound of it, but cannot tell where it comes from and where it goes. So is everyone who is born of the Spirit."* Therefore, the eagle Christians must be led by the wind of the Holy Spirit to fly to the destiny He has appointed for them to go to fulfill the perfect will of the Father God in their lives. If eagle Christians will go against the wind of the Holy Spirit, then they will create drag in their lives in such a way that it can open a door for the wind of the unclean spirit to blow at them.[38] If they keep going against the Spirit, then the wind of darkness will carry them away from the will of God and lead them into the whirlwind of bondage, destruction, and death.

The causes of the wind of the power of darkness will lead you to fulfill the lust of the eyes, the lust of the flesh, and the pride of life. You will bear the fruits in 1 Corinthians 6:9-10, "*Or **do you not know that the unrighteous will not inherit the kingdom of God**? Do not be deceived; neither the sexually immoral, nor idolaters, nor adulterers, nor homosexuals, nor thieves, nor the greedy, nor those habitually drunk, nor verbal abusers, nor swindlers, will inherit the kingdom of God.*" However, if they are led by the wind of the Holy Spirit, then the following seven blessings will follow them:

- **The wind of the Spirit blows them in the direction of holiness and purity**: Leviticus 20:26 commands, "*And you shall be holy to Me, for I the LORD am holy, and have separated you from the peoples, that you should be Mine.*" If eagle Christians are led by the wind of the Holy Spirit, then they will be separated unto the Lord for His holy purpose to accomplish His divine mission on earth.

- **The wind of the Holy Spirit blows in the direction of making God's children to be His new creations**: 2 Corinthians 5:17 declares, "*Therefore, if anyone is in Christ, he is a new creation; old things have passed away; behold, all things have become new.*" The wind of the Spirit will lead eagle Christians to be assured that their old ways of living in the bondages of sin and the devil has been terminated by the blood of the Lamb. As the resurrected Lord Jesus Christ and the power of the Holy Spirit indwell them, they have totally become new creations in the Lord.

Their sins have been removed as far as the East is from the West. The proof of that has been fulfilled in Romans 8:1-2, Romans 8:1-2, *"**There is therefore now no condemnation to those who are in Christ Jesus**, who do not walk according to the flesh, but according to the Spirit.* ***For the law of the Spirit of life in Christ Jesus has made me free from the law of sin and death.****"*

- **The wind of the Holy Spirit blows in the direction where the fruit of the Spirit will manifest**: Galatians 5:22-23 defines, *"But the fruit of the Spirit is love, joy, peace, longsuffering, kindness, goodness, faithfulness, gentleness, self-control. Against such there is no law."* If eagle Christians are led by the wind of the Holy Spirit, then they will produce and manifest the fruit of the Spirit whatever they are called to do or to go through. They will not be led by the character of the devil any longer, which is the complete opposite of the fruit of the Spirit.

- **The wind of the Holy Spirit blows in the direction where the children of God will arise to shine His light into the dark world**: Isaiah 60:1-2 directs, *"Arise, shine; For your light has come! And the glory of the LORD is risen upon you. For behold, the darkness shall cover the earth, And deep darkness the people; But the LORD will arise over you, And His* *glory will be seen upon you.*" Eagle Christians will arise and shine the glory of the Lord led by the wind of the Holy Spirit into this dark world. They will be able to lead many lost souls to the Kingdom of God, to heal the sick, and to bring deliverance to those who are under the bondages of the devil.

- **The wind of the Holy Spirit blows in the direction of empowering the children of God with His kingdom authority and power to destroy the works of the devil**: 1 John 3:8 declares, "*He who sins is of the devil, for the devil has sinned from the beginning. For this purpose the Son of God was manifested, that He might destroy the works of the devil.*" For eagle Christians to destroy the works of the devil, they must know how to move in the authority of Christ and the power of the Holy Spirit.

  Jesus Christ proclaimed in Matthew 28:18, "*And Jesus came and spoke to them saying, 'All authority has been given to me in heaven and on earth.'*" Since then, Jesus Christ dwells in you with all authority. Also, Acts 1:8 proclaims, "*But **you will receive power when the Holy Spirit comes upon you**. And you will be my witnesses, telling people about me everywhere—in Jerusalem, throughout Judea, in Samaria, and to the ends of the earth.*" (NLT)

  Thus, the Holy Spirit indwells you with the power of the Kingdom of God. Therefore, as the Lord wills, eagle Christians can move in the authority of Jesus Christ and the power of the Holy Spirit to destroy the works of the devil wherever they fly. In the book of Acts, the disciples of Christ moved with the wind of the Holy Spirit to save the lost, heal the sick, cleanse the lepers, cast out demons, and raise the dead (Matt. 10:7-8).

- **The wind of the Holy Spirit blows to raise the final harvest forces to finish the Great Commission**: Matthew 9:37-38 declares, *"The harvest truly is plentiful, but the laborers are few. Therefore, pray the Lord of the harvest to send out laborers into His harvest."* As the wind of the Holy Spirit blows upon eagle Christians, they will be directed to engage in making the Great Commission become the Great Completion in this generation as the final harvest forces.

    Because Matthew 24:14 has to be fulfilled in order for Jesus Christ to come back and the end of this age to be terminated, *"And the Good News about the Kingdom will be preached throughout the whole world, so that all nations will hear it; and then the end will come."* When the last Unreached People Group hears the gospel of Jesus Christ, then the end will come and Christ will return to initiate the millennial reign of the Kingdom of Heaven on earth with the saints (Revelation 20:1-4).

- **The wind of the Holy Spirit blows to make eagle Christians to become more than conquerors in Christ**: Eagle Christians who are led by the wind of the Spirit will be more than conquerors no matter how the devil might attack them, because they are securely anchored in the love of Jesus Christ according to Romans 8:37-39, *"Yet in all these things we are more than conquerors through Him who loved us. For I am persuaded that neither death nor life, nor angels nor* *principalities nor powers, nor things present nor things to come, nor height nor depth, nor any other created thing, shall be able to separate us from the love of God which is in Christ Jesus our Lord.*" Even death cannot separate eagle Christians from the love of Christ, because they will live with Him in heaven immediately after their lives are over in this life. Praise the Lord! No weapon formed against them shall prosper. If God is for them, who can be against them.

As you finish reading this book, you can become an Eagle Christian for God's glory. Please pray the following prayer out loud and declare that you will soar up high led by the wind of the Holy Spirit every moment of your life:

"Dear Lord, Jesus Christ, I repent of all my sins and ask you to come into my heart to be my Lord and Savior. Thank you for dying on the cross to take away my sins, sicknesses, curses, fear of death, and the power of Satan over my life. I surrender my conscious, sub-conscious, and unconscious minds to you and receive the mind of Christ in faith to guide my life according to the perfect will of the Father. Please write my name in the Book of Life. Fill me with the Holy Spirit and cause me to be totally led by the wind of the Holy Spirit to fulfill your creation mandate for my life. Help me to win many souls for the kingdom of God. Empower me to heal the sick and to destroy the works of the devil over multitudes of souls from my own Jerusalem to the end of the earth. I will be more than a conqueror in Christ. I am a born-again Eagle Christian now. In the mighty name of Jesus Christ, I pray. Amen!"

REFERENCES

---

[1] Derek Prince (1985). *Receiving God's Best* (P. 16-17). New Kensington, PA: Whitaker House.

[2] Thomas Nelson (2007). *The Ultimate Checklist for life* (P. 126). Nashville, TN: Thomas Nelson.

[3] Derek Prince (1987). *The Holy Spirit in You* (P. 69). Springdale, PA: Whitaker House.

[4] D. L. Moody (1997). *Secret Power* (P. 38). New Kensington, PA: Whitaker House.

[5] Derek Prince (1990). *Blessing or Curse, You can choose!* (P. 18): Tarrytown, NY: Chosen Books.

[6] Paul M. Goulet (2007). *The 5 Powers of God* (P. 71-72). Nashville, TN: Thomas Nelson.

[7] Don Gossett (1976). *Praise Avenue* (P. 106). Springdale, PA: Whitaker House.

[8] Charles Spurgeon (1993). *Spiritual Warfare in a Believer's Life* (P. 120-121). Lynnwood, WA: Emerald Books.

[9] Ernest J. Gruen (1976). *Freedom to Choose* (P. 104-105). Springdale, PA: Whitaker House.

[10] A. W. Tozer (1961). *The Knowledge of The Holy* (P. 49). New York, NY: Harper & Row, Publishers.

[11] Infoplease Staff (2023, January 16). *Major Military Operations Since World War II*: https://www.infoplease.com/history/us/major-military-operations-since-world-war-ii

[12] The World Counts (2023, March). *How Many People Die From Hunger Each Year?*: https://www.theworldcounts.com/challenges/people-and-poverty/hunger-and-obesity/how-many-people-die-from-hunger-each-year

[13] Hannah Ritchie, Pablo Rosado and Max Roser (2022). *Natural Disasters*: https://ourworldindata.org/natural-disasters#

[14] Linda Poon (2015, October 9). *Mapping 100 Years of Earthquakes, in 3-D – Bloomberg*: https://www.bloomberg.com/news/articles/2015-10-09/mapping-100-years-of-earthquakes-in-3d#

[15] Cath Martin (2014, June 25). *70 million Christians martyred for their faith since Jesus walked the earth*: https://www.christiantoday.com/article/70-million-christians-martyred-faith-since-jesus-walked-earth/38403.htm

[16] ChristianPost.com / Fox News (2017, July 6). *Nearly 1 million Christians reportedly martyred for their faith in last decade*: https://www.foxnews.com/world/ nearly-1-million-christians-reportedly-martyred-for-their-faith-in-last-decade

[17] The staff of Watchman Fellowship, Inc. *Index of Cults and Religions*: https://www.watchman.org/index-of-cults-and-religions/

[18] Joseph Kiprop (2017, July 9). *The Worst Decades For Crime*: https://www.worldatlas.com/articles/which-decade-had-the-most-crime.html

[19] Joshua Project (2023). *Frontier Unreached Peoples*: https://www.joshuaproject.net/frontier

[20] *Secret Power* (Moody, 1997, P. 65)

[21] Kendall K. Morgan (2022, June 19). *How Many People Die of Cancer a Year?*: https://www.webmd.com/cancer/how-many-cancer-deaths-per-year

[22] Center for Disease Control and Prevention (2022, October 4). *Disease Burden of Flu*: https://www.cdc.gov/flu/about/burden/index.html

[23] Worldometer's COVID-19 data (2024, April 13). *Coronavirus Cases*: https://www.worldometers.info/coronavirus/country/us/

[24] *Frontier Unreached Peoples* (Joshua Project, 2023)

[25] Paul Borthwick (2012). *Western Christians in Global Mission* (P. 112-113). Downers Grove, IL: IVP Books

[26] Kenneth Copeland (2018, May 24). *How to Experience Signs, Wonders, and Miracles*: https://blog.kcm.org/experience-signs-wonders-miracles/

[27] Charles Finney (1996). *Power from God* (P. 9-10). New Kensington, PA: Whitaker House

[28] Open Doors (2023). *How are Christians persecuted in Bhutan?*: https://www.opendoorsuk.org/persecution/world-watch-list/bhutan/

[29] Paul Yonggi Cho (1984). *The Leap of Faith* (P. 37). South Plainfield, NJ: Bridge Publishing, Inc.

[30] Charles Spurgeon (1993). *Spiritual Warfare in a Believer's Life* (P. 160). Lynnwood, WA: Emerald Books

[31] Guillermo Maldonado (2011). *How to Walk in the Supernatural Power of God* (P. 167). New Kensington, PA: Whitaker House

[32] *The Holy Spirit in You* (Prince, 1987, P. 18-19)

[33] Smith Wigglesworth (1999). *Healing* (P. 136). New Kensington, PA: Whitaker House

[34] Bibles for Europe (2017, November 10). *Three Greek Words for Life in the New Testament and How They Apply to Us*: https://blog.biblesforeurope.org/three-greek-words-for-life-in-the-new-testament-and-how-they-apply-to-us/

[35] Wildlife Informer (2023). *Characteristics of Eagles (8 Examples)*: https://wildlifeinformer.com/characteristics-of-eagles/

[36] Nirjla Rana (2016, August 29). *Seven Leadership Principles To Learn From An Eagle*: https://www.linkedin.com/pulse/seven-leadership-principles-learn-from-eagle-nira-nirjla-rana

[37] Avian Report (2023). *The Bald Eagle Wingspan: How does it compare to other Birds of Prey?*: https://avianreport.com/bald-eagle-wingspan-versus-birds-prey/

[38] Jonathan Cahn (2016). *The Book of Mysteries* (P. 62). Lake Mary, FL: FrontLine Charisma Media/Charisma House Book Group

ABOUT THE AUTHOR AND HIS MINISTRIES

.Dr. James Lee is the Founder and President of River of Life Ministries, whose mission is to equip indigenous Christian leaders through establishing the River Missions Training Centers (RMTCs) and conducting the Global Harvest Network (GHN) Conferences to plant indigenous churches among the Unreached People Groups in the world. He is also the Founder and President of Door of Hope Foundation, which carries out God's divine mission to bring the hope of Jesus Christ to facilitate charitable works that will enhance the welfare of the neediest and most vulnerable children and people in the world.

In 1985, Dr. Lee received the call to become a full-time minister while stationed in the Flying Squadron 2 of NATO AWACS base in Germany as a senior Captain in the U.S. Air Force. Since he resigned his commission from the Air Force in 1987, he received his Master of Arts in World Missions and a Doctor of Ministry degree in Global Evangelization from Regent University in Virginia Beach, Virginia. Since 1988, Dr. Lee has traveled to more than 100 countries spreading the Gospel of Jesus Christ to multitudes of unreached people groups. He has equipped indigenous disciples through establishing RMTCs and conducting GHN Conferences. His disciples have planted over 800 indigenous churches worldwide. Dr. Lee is an apostle to the nations, an equipper of disciples, and an anointed evangelist with signs, wonders and miracles following in his ministries.

OTHER BOOKS BY DR. JAMES LEE

When God Walks with an Ordinary Man—A book which will inspire all believers in Christ to trust Him with all their hearts by allowing Him to walk with them to achieve His plan and purpose in their lives for His glory. God can empower His ordinary sons and daughters with His divine authority and power to accomplish His extraordinary tasks on earth as His special agents. In this book, Dr. Lee shares his divine encounters with supernatural God during his many missions' trips in the world. As you read this book, God will increase your faith so you can also do His divine works with signs, wonders and miracles following.

The Kingdom of Heaven is at Hand—Every believer in Yeshua the Messiah must understand God's overall mission for fallen mankind. Once the disciples of Christ truly grasp God's heart for the Israelites and the Gentiles, they must walk with the authority of Yeshua and the power of the Holy Spirit, demonstrating His kingdom presence in this dark world.

God's core mission is to utilize the Israelites to bring His Salvation and Kingdom Plans to bless all the families of the earth through the Son of the living God, Yeshua. The invisible Kingdom of Heaven has touched down on the Day of Pentecost. When this Gospel of the Kingdom is preached throughout the world, witnessing to all the families of the earth, then the end will come…

It is Written—Spiritual Warfare must be focused on God and His mighty power. The battle belongs to the Lord! As believers in Christ, we must focus on God's divine authority and power to destroy the works of the devil by evangelizing the world. When we engage in all sorts of spiritual battles in life, we must focus on becoming strong in the Lord and in the power of His might (Ephesians 6:10). We must not focus on Satan and his evil hosts of darkness. In this book, Dr. Lee examines the Scriptures to see how the heroes of the faith conducted spiritual warfare so we can learn from their examples how to apply their principles to our own spiritual battles.

CONTACT INFORMATION

If God has made this book a blessing to you and you wish to share a testimony, or if you wish to be on the River of Life Ministries' mailing list to become a partner and receive our monthly newsletter, write to:

River of Life Ministries
P. O. Box 6128
Virginia Beach, VA 23456-0128
Web: www.rlmva.org
E-mail: riveroflife@rlmva.org
Tel: 757-554-0053

If you wish to support orphans and needy children in the world, then write to:

Door of Hope Foundation
P. O. Box 6261
Virginia Beach, VA 23456-0261
Web: www.doorofhopefoundation.com
E-mail: dhf@doorofhopefoundation.com
Tel: 757-271-6755

ISBN 978-1-7342549-7-6

$15.00

51500>

www.ingramcontent.com/pod-product-compliance
Lightning Source LLC
Chambersburg PA
CBHW051831090426
42736CB00011B/1745